Concise Guide to
Technical and Academic Writing

Praise for
Concise Guide to Technical and Academic Writing

For a PhD candidate and a novice to academic writing like myself, this guide was extremely useful. The sections on knowing your reader and style, and the advice for direct and concise writing were particularly useful. I would recommend this to anyone commencing a higher degree!

Deme, Amazon review

In this guide, Bowman provides those of us who write for academic audiences a cogent, effective guide to good, clear writing. He offers a straightforward guide to achieving the goal of the book, which, he says, is to help readers to write well. Where other guides might overwhelm writers with detail, Bowman's . . . spares unnecessary discussion and illustrates convincingly why certain principles are necessary for effective writing.

D. Bunn Jr., PhD student, Fuller Theological Seminary, Amazon review

In thirty-plus years of teaching English, ten of them at the college level, I've never seen a clearer, more focused presentation of the basic concepts needed to produce readable writing. When I taught freshman composition at a state university, the assigned English text contained 894 pages, not counting a glossary and index. I wish I'd had David Bowman's *Concise Guide to Academic and Technical Writing* instead.

In just 124 pages, David Bowman succeeds in packing all the grammatical and structural information a writer of technical or academic texts needs to produce a workmanlike product. Not a word is wasted on irrelevancies; only the information needed to write objective, coherent, uncluttered informational prose is included.

Maeve Maddox, Ph.D., the American English Doctor, educator, and author

Also by David Bowman

300 Days of Better Writing

300 top strategies for writing clearly, persuasively, and directly.

Bang! Writing with Impact

114 strategies in 18 categories to make your readers pay attention.

Precise Edit Training Manual

The 29 most common strategies we use and the problems we fix.

Which Word Do I Use?

The 26 most commonly mistaken word pairs, fully explained so you can use the correct word and say what you mean.

Writing Tips for a Year

Receive a new writing tip, strategy, resource, or piece of advice— every day for an entire year.

Zen Comma

Zen Comma, an e-book in PDF and Kindle formats, examines the 17 major uses and misuses of commas.

More information and samples:
http://HostileEditing.com

Concise Guide to Technical and Academic Writing

David Bowman

Write Well Publishing

Published by Write Well Publishing

978-0-9885078-2-1

About the book

How many times have I heard, "This is technical writing—it's not supposed to be good writing"? How many times have I heard, "This is a dissertation—it's supposed to sound *academic*"? Answer: Too many times.

Academic and technical documents present focused information to a targeted audience. Technical and academic writiers, in their attempt to provide professional-sounding writing, too often lose sight of the fact that someone will read what they write. And this means the writing needs to be clear, logically organized, and engaging.

Technical writing and academic writing can be good writing. The purpose of this writing guide is to help academic and technical writers produce good writing.

About the author

David Bowman specializes in writing well. With over 20 years of editing experience, Mr. Bowman has a wealth of strategies and advice to help you communicate in writing, connect with your reader, and reach your goals.

David Bowman is the author of 7 books on writing, the popular *Precise Edit Training Manual*, *300 Days of Better Writing*, *Zen Comma*, *Which Word Do I Use?*, *Bang! Writing with Impact*, *Concise Guide to Technical and Academic Writing*, and *Your Writing Companion*. In addition to serving as the chief editor of Precise Edit, he is a writing instructor for the University of New Mexico and private writing coach and consultant for many organizations.

Mr. Bowman knows that all people need to write well: it's how we communicate with each other. However, writing is an overlooked skill. He writes books on writing so that others may learn to write—and edit—like a professional. These are more than books on grammar and punctuation. These are books on effective communication through writing.

TABLE OF CONTENTS

TABLE OF TABLES

TABLE OF FIGURES

SECTION A: CENTRAL CONCEPTS OF TECHNICAL WRITING

1. INTRODUCTION TO TECHNICAL WRITING

A. What is Technical Writing?

The Society of Technical Writers describes technical writers as people who "research and create information about technical processes or products directed to a targeted audience through various forms of media." This description touches on two foundations of technical writing: *information* and *targeted audience*. With this in mind, technical writing is far more than creating user manuals.

Technical writing is an *approach* to presenting information to a defined reader in an objective, direct, easy-to-understand manner. Technical writing is a strategy for providing information in an easy-to-use manner. In other words, technical writing is good writing.

Based on this understanding of technical writing, technical writing applies to many types of documents. Although technical writing is for user manuals and product descriptions, it is also used for

- project reports,
- white papers,
- information presentations,
- instructional texts,
- position papers, and
- annual reports.

B. What is Academic Writing?

Academic writing, too, is an *approach* to providing information to a targeted audience, whether a professor, subscribers to a professional journal, or a dissertation committee. Academic writing provides clear information that is focused on a specific topic and organized to present ideas logically. Like technical writing, academic writing is good writing.

Samples of academic writing include

- dissertations and theses,
- expository essays,
- book and article reviews, and
- research findings.

C. Principles of Technical & Academic Writing

Technical and academic writing follow several principles.

- The reader is more important than the writer.
- The style must be consistent with the purpose.
- Clear, simple writing increases understanding.
- Logical organization shows how ideas connect.
- The reader needs to know how to find information.
- Information sources must be given credit.
- Correct grammar, punctuation, and word choice enhance credibility.

The purpose of this book is to help you implement these principles and write well.

2. THE READER

A. Identify the Reader

The reader is more important than the writer, i.e., you. Before you can determine what to write, how to write it, and how to present it, you must determine who will read it.

In many cases, you may know the *actual person* who will read your document (such as your boss, your professor, the company owner, the project head, the contracting officer). In other cases, you may know the *type of person* who will read your document (such as company shareholders, organization decision-makers, buyers of a product, policy makers, purchasing agents, mid-level managers).

Define that person with the statement, "This will be read by . . . ." Once you have done so, you can begin to mold your document to the reader's needs.

B. Understand the Readers' Needs

Readers have needs. You don't create those needs. Your job is to satisfy them. Whether consciously or unconsciously, when readers pick up your document, they are thinking, "Give me what I want and don't waste my time."

At the same time, you have a purpose. You want to accomplish something with your document, such as an action by the reader, something that benefits you directly, or something that encourages further communication.

You will only accomplish your purpose by helping the readers satisfy their needs.

The central question is "What does my reader want from this document?" The better you understand your readers' characteristics, the more likely you are to accomplish your purpose.

David Bowman

Readers' characteristics include the following:

- interests, goals, purpose;
- desired information;
- prior knowledge of topic;
- prior relationship (with you, your organization, etc.);
- communication style;
- amount of time for reading;
- patience, tolerance, and confidence;
- simultaneous actions; and
- familiarity with the jargon.

C. Address Your Readers' Needs

Communication is the key to achieving your purpose. Your job is to make sure your document's characteristics align with the readers' characteristics. Knowledge of the reader will help you communicate effectively.

3. STYLE

Writing style comprises four characteristics:

1. Formality,
2. Language complexity,
3. Objectivity, and
4. Information depth.

The purpose you are trying to accomplish, the readers' needs, your relationship with the reader, and the type of document affect the style in which you write. Style is a strategy for effective writing, not a goal.

A. Formality

Formality means (1) the degree to which you use standard English conventions, real and assumed, (2) the degree to which you use common words, as opposed to colloquial, idiomatic words, (3) the size and type of audience you address, and (4) the nature of the relationship you assume with the reader.

Levels of formality, sometimes called language registers, can be construed as follows.

Intimate (least formal):

Who: best friends or significant others

Requires: shared experiences, understanding of common topics, shared definitions of what specific words and expressions mean (which may be different or more specific than used by the general public)

Standards: does not reflect Standard English conventions of grammar or sentence structure

Use: only when speaking or writing to people in your closest relationships, implies social and emotional closeness

Casual:

Who: people with whom you associate casually, e.g., friends and family members, frequent acquaintances.

Requires: shared experiences, common interests, similar personalities

Standards: Word use is often idiosyncratic (i.e., slang).

Note: Although this language register has been described as "friendly" language, we may also use casual language in unfriendly circumstances. Casual language depends on your relationship with the other person.

Social:

Who: appropriate for most social encounters; people you meet in social situations, such as a shop clerk, a new acquaintance, or the friend of a friend

Requires: does not depend on shared experiences but may employ idioms common to a particular community or culture

Standards: broadly accepted word definitions, common yet respectful ways of addressing the other person, standard English conventions (though not as rigorously as more formal registers)

Use: implies membership within a particular community or general culture, appropriate if you are trying to establish yourself as a member of a particular social community

Formal:

Who: people you communicate with in a professional environment, people with whom you don't have any social connection (or when the social connection is irrelevant), recipients of disseminated professional information

Requires: broadly accepted word definitions, doesn't assume the reader has shared experiences or any social connection to the writer or speaker

Standards: rigorously follows standard English conventions; avoids personal opinions, feelings, and most experiences from private life

Use: This is the most acceptable level for most published or broadly disseminated documents, business documents, and academic documents.

Professional:

Who: members of a specific profession, technical field, or academic field; a specific, targeted group of readers in a professional field

Requires: common professional language with specific words and expressions (i.e., jargon), specific expertise in a field of study, shared expertise and experience within a particular professional field

Standards: rigorously follows standards English conventions

Use: published or public documents for other members of the professional field

The general appropriateness of each formality level is as follows.

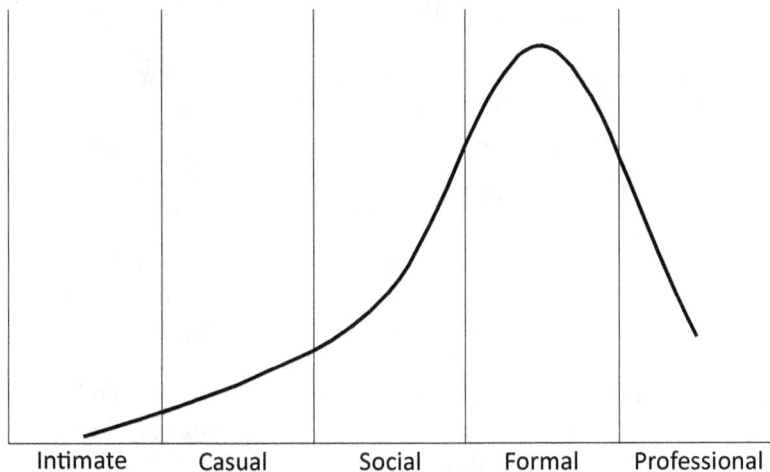

| Intimate | Casual | Social | Formal | Professional |

Figure 1. Acceptability and frequency of formality levels for business professionals and students: a rough comparison.

This examination of formality levels is useful for two reasons.

1. It may help you select and use the appropriate level. If you use a level that is too intimate, you presume a level of intimacy that the reader does not share. If you use a level that is too formal, you may be perceived as an arrogant, condescending outsider. In either case, you damage the relationship with the reader that you need to accomplish your purposes.

2. Understanding various levels of formality will help you gauge the effectiveness of your communications, make adjustments, and become flexible in your communication style.

Although the formality levels address word usage, nothing about the formal or professional writing indicates that using longer, more esoteric words is better. In fact, if certain words are not common to the audience you are addressing, or if you are unsure about how they are used, you risk damaging your communication and credibility.

In business, school, and most professional environments, effective writing stays firmly within the formal level unless you have a very specific, considered reason to use a different level.

B. Language Complexity

Some writers use straightforward sentences with few modifying phrases and clauses. Others use complex sentences with many modifiers, interjected descriptions, and multiple clauses and phrases.

> *Example B.1, simple sentence:* "Lisa bought a red car."

This simple sentence contains a simple subject (*Lisa*) and a simple predicate with an object (*bought a red car*). This sentence has two modifying words (*a, red*) but no other phrases or clauses.

> *Example B.2, moderately complex sentence:* "When the day ended, Lisa, a sales clerk at the downtown market, bought a red car."

This moderately complex sentence has an introductory descriptive clause (*when the day ended*), a simple subject (*Lisa*), an appositive for the subject (*a sales clerk at the downtown market*), and a simple predicate with an object (*bought a red car*).

> *Example B.3, very complex sentence:* "When the day ended, which couldn't have happened soon enough, given the type of day she had had, Lisa, a sales clerk at the downtown market, a grimy, dark nook in an old building, bought what she mistakenly thought was a new, or, at the worst, slightly used, red car."

This very complex sentence has an introductory descriptive clause (*when the day ended*), a description of the introductory clause (*which couldn't have happened soon enough*), a description of the description of the introductory clause (*given the type of day she had had*), a subject (*Lisa*), an appositive for the subject (*a sales clerk at the downtown market*), a description of the appositive for the subject (*a grimy, dark nook*), and a description of the description of the appositive for the subject (*in an old building*). And then we finally get to the predicate, which is similarly complicated.

As these three examples show, the two key features of language complexity are

1.   the number of descriptive phases and clauses and
2.   the levels of description (such as description of description).

A careful writer considers sentence complexity in light of the readers' needs. Simple sentences can be read quickly and understood easily. As sentences become more complex, they contain more information and "flavor," but they require more work from the readers and increase the potential for misunderstanding.

As with all style issues, the level of language complexity needs to fit the readers' needs. Simple sentences are the most easy to understand. They present minimal information in a straightforward manner, with no interruptions in the main thought being communicated. On the other hand, using too many simple sentences, or a string of simple sentences, makes the writing appear amateurish.

For technical manuals, lists of instructions, user guides, and other documents that present single action steps, stick with simple sentences. For most other types of documents, the writer can present more complex information and create better reader interest and engagement by using a mix of simple and moderately complex sentences. If your goal is reader understanding and interest, avoid very complex sentences. Overall, you will communicate best by

- using a mix of simple and moderately complex sentences,
- limiting the number of descriptive phrases,
- presenting only one descriptive phrase at a time, and
- avoiding descriptions of descriptions.

Sentence structure will be addressed in greater detail in Chapter 6, Sentence Structure.

C. Objectivity

Feelings, emotions, opinions, and beliefs are called, collectively, *individual perspective*. An individual perspective indicates the perspective of one person: the writer. In all forms of technical writing, your individual perspective is inappropriate.

Think about your reader. Your reader is seeking believable, credible information. Your opinions, etc. are not believable, credible information. They only apply to you; they do not apply to your reader.

The most obvious cases are sentence that contain such phrases as *I feel that*, *I believe*, and *in my opinion*. If you can express the idea as a fact, do so. If you cannot express the idea without those phrases, remove the sentence entirely.

Writers also interject their individual perspectives by using particular words and by making judgments, as explained below.

Word choice: Writers damage the objectivity of their writing (and its value) by using adjectives and adverbs that indicate an individual perspective. For example, these two sentences contain opinions:

Example C.1: "The marketing plan indicates exciting opportunities for the company."

Example C.2: "The friendly sales associates will greet our valued customers by name."

In these samples, the words indicating the individual perspective are *exciting, friendly,* and *valued.*

Some words indicate individual perspectives with greater subtlety through their connotative meanings. The connotation of a word implies more than the objective meaning of the word. This not only increases the likelihood for misunderstanding but also reflects the writer's opinion. For example:

Example C.3: "Rescue crews sorted through the carnage from the plane crash."

Here, *carnage* implies the writer's impression of the scene. It evokes visions of war or disaster. A more objective word is *wreckage.*

Moral Judgments and Persuasion: A writer expresses an individual perspective by using such words as *should, must,* and *ought to.* (The technical term for this type of word is *modal auxiliary.*) In most cases, writers use these words to persuade the reader to act or think in a specific manner. This is a problem for several reasons.

First, these words will always create conflict with the reader. They communicate your belief that you have the right to tell the reader what to do. The reader is unlikely to share that belief. Second, they state an opinion as a moral judgment. Moral or otherwise, an opinion is still just that: an opinion. The reader will recognize that you are providing your opinion and can, therefore, reject your ideas. Third, they disrespect the reader. They communicate that you don't trust the reader to decide what to do.

As a persuasion technique, this rarely works. In technical writing, it is inappropriate. A better approach is to state ideas as facts and to connect the facts to a desired outcome. A reader can argue against, or reject, your opinions easily. However, the reader cannot argue against objective facts. In the following examples, example C.4a communicates an opinion, and example C.4b communicates a fact.

Example C.4a: "The WHO should provide funding for sanitation projects in third-world countries. This will reduce the incidence of diarrhea in third world countries."

Example C.4b: "The WHO will reduce the incidence of diarrhea in third world countries by providing funding for sanitation projects."

Example C.4a makes a moral judgment. In the writer's opinion, the WHO will do the "morally right" thing by providing funding. Example C.4b provides a fact. The reduction in incidences of diarrhea *will* occur if the WHO provides funding. Moral judgments create conflict. Facts persuade.

Personal Pronouns: Writing in an objective style does not mean avoiding *I* and *we*. These personal pronouns are acceptable if you are describing your actions or processes. You can write "We did this" or "I did that." This approach is preferable to writing such artificial phrases as "the author of this report found...." The reader knows that you are the author. Use *I*.

When you write *I* or *we*, examine your sentence critically and ask what you are communicating. If you are communicating a fact, the personal pronoun is acceptable. If you are communicating an opinion, it is not.

Describing Opinions: At times, you may need to provide opinions, feelings, and beliefs. It is possible to do so in an objective manner. Although you don't want to offer your own individual perspective, you can describe the individual perspective of others. For example, rather than stating

"I believe the president is doing a good job,"

you can state

"22% of survey respondents believed the president is doing a good job"

or

"The president believed he was doing a good job."

In this way, you are simply providing the facts about others' opinions. That other people believe, feel, etc. this way is a fact. Technical writing is not about you, but it can be about other people.

D. Information Depth

Information depth means how much information you provide about a topic. As in all cases, think about the reader. Two questions will help you determine the appropriate information depth:

1. What does the reader already know?
2. How much information does the reader need?

Technical writing is based on the principle that every word must have value to the reader, and this principle relates to information depth. If you don't give the reader sufficient information, you are not satisfying the reader's needs, and the reader will look elsewhere for information. If you give the reader more information than needed, you may bore the reader, appear condescending, or make it difficult for the reader to find the information needed.

For example, let's say you are describing research findings. Other researchers, journal editors, and dissertation committee members will want to know the specific steps you took to gather and analyze the data. They want to know whether the process is valid so they can judge the merits of the findings. On the other hand, if you are preparing a white paper on the policy implications of the findings, information about your methodology may not be needed. Policy makers may be satisfied if you state that you used a rigorous, credible methodology. They are more interested in what you discovered and how it affects their decisions.

Writers passionate about their topics tend to provide too much information or the wrong information because they don't know what the reader wants. Writers who focus on their own knowledge of the topic tend to provide too little because they can leave out much of the information and still understand their writing. As with any style issue, therefore, the first step is to think about the reader.

SECTION B: ESSENTIAL WRITING STRATEGIES

4. DIRECT WRITING

A. The Basic Concept

Direct writing gives the readers what they want in an economical, straightforward manner without filler or unnecessary complexity. Direct writing presents information clearly and efficiently, thus providing the answer to the question readers ask of every sentence: "Who did what to whom?"

The key components of this question are as follows.

- **Who:** Who or what is doing the action described in the sentence? In direct writing, the answer to this question is the *subject* of the sentence.
- **What:** What action is occurring? In direct writing, the answer to this question is the *main verb* of the sentence.
- **To whom or to what:** What did the subject do the action to? The answer to this question is the *object*. Not every sentence will have an object.

These key components are the foundation of the discussion on direct writing. Examples A.1 and A.2 demonstrate how these components are used.

Example A.1: "Veterinarians have discovered a new form of feline leukemia."
Who (subject): *veterinarians*
Did what (main verb): *have discovered*
To whom/what (object): *a new form of feline leukemia*

Example A.2: "Fourteen members of Congress changed party affiliation during the campaign."
Who (subject): *fourteen members of Congress*
Did what (main verb): *changed*
To whom/what (object): *party affiliation*

When the reader can answer "Who did what to whom?" the reader will understand your idea. In direct writing, the subject (who?) and main verb (did what?) communicate the main point of the sentence.

This concept has two implications, as follows:

1. The subject and main verb must be obvious to the reader, and
2. Direct writing uses carefully chosen subjects and verbs.

Thus, the first question to ask when writing or revising is "What are the subject and main verb?" The most important revision strategies depend on the answer to this question. With this in mind, the discussion on direct writing focuses on subjects and verbs and answering the readers' question.

B. Subjects

The subject of the sentence focuses the readers' attention because it answers the question "Who?" The writer is telling the reader, "This is what the sentence is about." Because the subject of the sentence is so important, direct writing requires the writer to choose the subject carefully.

Grammatical and Meaningful Subjects: A sentence has two types of subjects: the grammatical subject and the meaningful subject.

The *grammatical subject* is the word or phrase in the subject's position, typically before the main verb. It serves the grammatical role of subject and determines what the main verb will be. In examples A.1 and A.2 above, the grammatical subjects are *veterinarians* and *fourteen members of Congress*, respectively. These are the words before the main verb (i.e., *have discovered, changed*), and they determine what the main verb will be. They serve the grammatical function of the subject, so they are called the grammatical subject. Every complete sentence has at least one grammatical subject.

When you ask the question, "What are the subject and main verb?" you identify the grammatical subject.

The concept of a *meaningful subject* is more complex. The meaningful subject is what the sentence is supposed to be about. To find the meaningful subject, the writer can ask what action the sentence describes. Once we identify the main action, we ask who or what is doing that action. The answer will be the meaningful subject. We can use a previous example to understand this concept better.

> *Example B.1:* "Veterinarians have discovered a new form of feline leukemia."
> **Main action:** discovering a new form of feline leukemia
> **Who or what is doing the main action:** *veterinarians*
> **Meaningful subject:** *veterinarians*

Example B.1 is about *veterinarians*, making *veterinarians* the meaningful subject.

In direct writing, the meaningful subject is always the same as the grammatical subject. After answering "What are the subject and main action of the sentence?" the writer needs to ask "Is the sentence about the subject?" If the answer is Yes, then the grammatical subject and the meaningful subject are the same. However, if the answer is No, then the sentence needs to be revised, as seen in example B.2.

> *Example B.2:* "There is concern about the new policy among safety officers."
> **Grammatical subject:** *there* (the subject of the main verb *is*)
> **Main action:** having concerns
> **Who or what is doing the main action:** *safety officers*
> **Meaningful subject:** safety officers

In this poorly written sentence, the meaningful subject (*safety officers*) is not the same as the grammatical subject (*there*). To revise this sentence, we can use the meaningful subject as the grammatical subject, leading to the following revision:

> "Safety officers have concerns about the new policy."

The revised sentence exemplifies direct writing because the grammatical and meaningful subjects are the same words. (On a side note, in every sentence that uses *there* as the grammatical subject, the grammatical and meaningful subjects will be different, and the sentence will need to be revised.)

Unlike example B.2, some sentences do not indicate who or what is the meaningful subject. The writer will need to consider the context of the sentence to determine the meaningful subject, as in the underlined sentence in example B.3.

> *Example B.3:* "Financial experts spent three weeks examining
> the company budget. <u>After careful analysis, the conclusion was
> that the company has sufficient funds for the project.</u>"
> **Grammatical subject:** *conclusion*
> **Main action:** concluding, reaching a conclusion
> **Who or what did the main action:** This sentence does not
> indicate who reached a conclusion, but the previous sentence
> suggests that it was the finance experts.
> **Meaningful subject:** *finance experts*

In this poorly written sentence, the meaningful subject (*finance experts*)
is not the same as the grammatical subject (*conclusion*). To revise this
sentence, we can use the meaningful subject as the grammatical
subject, leading to the following revision:

> "After careful analysis, finance experts concluded that the
> company has sufficient funds for the project."

Sometimes, when revising sentences to use the meaningful subject
as the grammatical subject, we have choices about what to make the
meaningful subject, and this brings us to the second issues about
subjects.

Choosing the Correct Meaningful Subject: The readers will focus
on whatever word or words you put in the subject position. This
means you can change the readers' attention and the emphasis in the
sentence by choosing different meaningful subjects.

The previous example shows how the focus changes depending on
the subject.

> *Example B.4a, original sentence:* "After careful analysis, the
> <u>conclusion</u> was that the company had sufficient funds for the
> project.
> *Example B.4b, revised, emphasis on the finance experts:* "After careful
> analysis, <u>finance experts</u> concluded that the company has
> sufficient funds for the project."
> *Example B.4c, revised, emphasis on the company:* "Based on a careful

analysis by finance experts, the <u>company</u> has sufficient funds for the project."

Example B.4d, revised, emphasis on the funds: "Based on a careful analysis of the company's finances, sufficient <u>funds</u> are available for the project.

As seen by these examples, the writer not only uses the meaningful subject as the grammatical subject but also determines the topic of the sentence, whether the finance experts (B.4b), the company (B.4c), or the funds (B.4d).

This brings us back to the readers' primary question: "Who did what to whom?" The word you choose as the subject answers *who*. As noted previously, the subject, main verb, and object carry the main message of the sentence; the rest is description. Thus, you can change the message of the sentence by using a different subject.

In direct writing, you write what you mean clearly and economically. You can only do this if you choose the subject that communicates the point you wish to make.

Subjects that Can Act: When deciding what the meaningful subject will be, you have three types of nouns from which to choose: creatures, things, and ideas.

- Creatures (e.g., people and animals) are the natural choice for subjects because they can act.
  Example: The <u>committee members</u> convened at 10:00 a.m.
- Things (e.g., inanimate objects and places) can do something, but in many cases they are acted upon.
  Example: The <u>projector</u> began smoking.
- Ideas (e.g., abstractions, concepts, and processes) cannot act. They exist and can be acted upon.
  Example: <u>Disagreement with committee decisions</u> is not welcome.

The readers' question "Who did what to whom?" implies that the subject is able to do something. For this reason, creatures make better subjects than things, and things make better subjects than ideas.

With a subject that can perform an action, and with that action described by the sentence, the sentence will be more interesting and will communicate more clearly. This gives you the opportunity to keep sharing your information. More importantly, the reader will be able to visualize the subject performing the action, increasing both understanding and remembrance.

Avoiding Anthropomorphism: *Anthropomorphism* is giving human qualities to non-human or conceptual subjects. Anthropomorphism is inaccurate writing that reflects sloppy thinking. As noted in the subsection immediately above, choose subjects that have the ability to perform the action.

Anthropomorphism can be weak or strong, as seen in examples B.5a and B.5b.

> *Example B.5a, weak anthropomorphism:* The municipal government acted to reduce crime rates.
> *Example B.5b, strong anthropomorphism:* The municipal government felt crime rates were too high.

Examples B.5a and B.5b both reflect sloppy thinking, but some readers may accept B.5a . The problem is that *government* is a concept, not a creature or thing. On the other hand, when policies or laws are created, the government, as a whole, can be described as "acting," even though the people who compose the government are the true actors. To be more accurate, example 5.Ba can be written "Municipal policy-makers acted to reduce crime rates" or "Local officials passed new regulations to reduce crime rates."

Example B.5b is a bigger problem. Although you could make the case that a company "acts," you can't claim that it "feels," implying emotions. Feeling is truly a human quality; hence, to say a company "feels" is clear anthropomorphism. To correct this example, we ask *who* is doing the main action and use the answer as the subject. Here, the municipal policy-makers, or officials, are feeling. Thus, we can correct the sentence as seen in example B.5c.

> *Example B.5c, no anthropomorphism:* Municipal policy-makers felt the crime rates were too high.

Here is a subtle example of anthropomorphism and its correction:

> *Example B.6a, anthropomorphism:* The research study attempted to identify causes of heart disease.
>
> *Example B.6b, no anthropomorphism:* In this study, the researchers attempted to identify causes of heart disease.

Notice in examples B.6 that a study is a concept and has neither desires nor goals. It cannot attempt something. However, researchers can, and they make the attempt by conducting their study.

C. Main Verbs

A sentence can have many verbs, but only one verb will be the main verb. The main verb begins the predicate of the sentence, which is the second part of the main message in a sentence. This verb answers the "did what" part of the readers' question, "Who did what do whom?"

Grammatical Main Verbs and Meaningful Actions: A sentence has two main types of verbs: The grammatical main verb and the meaningful action.

The *grammatical main verb* is the word in the position of the main verb. Because it has the grammatical role of main verb, it is called the grammatical main verb. It begins the predicate of the sentence and links with the grammatical subject. When you ask the question "What are the subject and main verb?" you identify the grammatical main verb, as seen in example C.1.

> *Example C.1:* "Fourteen members of Congress changed party affiliation during the campaign."
> **What is the subject?** *Fourteen members of Congress*
> **What is the verb linked to the subject?** *changed*
> **What is the grammatical main verb?** *changed*

The concept of the *meaningful action* is more complex. To find the meaningful action, the writer asks, "What is the main action being described in the sentence?" The answer will be the meaningful action, as seen in example C.2.

Example C.2: "Veterinarians have discovered a new form of feline leukemia."
Main action described by the sentence: discovering
Meaningful action: discovering

Direct writing uses the meaningful action as the grammatical main verb. After answering, "What are the subject and main verb?" the writer needs to ask, "Is the main verb also the main action being described?" If the answer is Yes, then the main verb and meaningful action are the same. If the answer is No, then the sentence needs to be revised.

The subject and the main verb communicate the primary message of the sentence. If you use the wrong verb, you divert the reader's attention from the message you intend. On the other hand, if you use the meaningful action as the main verb, you accurately communicate your message and direct the reader's attention to the point you wish to make. Example C.3 demonstrates how the grammatical main verb and meaningful action may be different.

Example C.3: "Free energy sources are what politicians describe as science fiction."
Grammatical main verb: *are* (following the grammatical subject *free energy sources*)
Main action described by the sentence: describing
Meaningful action: describing

Here, the main verb (*are*) differs from the meaningful action (*describing*). To revise this sentence, we use the meaningful action as the grammatical main verb, leading to the following revision:

"Politicians describe free energy sources as science fiction."

When writers use the meaningful action as the grammatical main verb, they will also use the meaningful subject as the grammatical subject. The revised sentence describes politicians and their actions, and it uses *politicians* as the grammatical subject.

As discussed above in "Choosing the Correct Meaningful Subject," a writer can choose different subjects to change the focus of the sentence. If we want this sentence to be about *free energy sources*, we can instead write

"Free energy sources are science fiction, politicians claim"

or

"According to politicians, free energy sources are science fiction."

These two options, with *free energy sources* as the subject, use *are* as the main verb. This approach is risky because *are* is a state-of-being verb, not an action verb. To understand why this is risky, we turn next to action verbs and state-of-being verbs.

Action Verbs and State-of-being Verbs: All verbs fall into these two broad categories.

Action verbs describe something happening, something changing, something progressing, something using energy. In brief, they describe actions. Although some actions are invisible (e.g., *thinking, forgetting*), all actions are something that happens.

In contrast, state-of-being verbs describe what something is. Nothing happens. Things simply are. These are also called *linking verbs* because they link something to its description. If we were to represent a sentence mathematically, we would represent state-of-being verbs as equal signs.

Table 1: Sample Action Verbs and State-of-Being Verbs

Sample Action Verbs	Sample State-of-being verbs
discuss, state, find, describe, note, write, send, pay, illustrate, attach	is, are, was, were, become, am, appears, tastes (not the action of sampling), feels (not the action of touching)

The first sample below uses an action verb, and the second sample uses a state-of-being verb.

Example C.4: "Personnel managers <u>facilitate</u> solutions to company disputes."

Example C.5: "Social media tools <u>are</u> useful." (i.e., social media tools = useful)

Direct writing relies mainly on action verbs. Action verbs provide information and contribute to the main idea being expressed. Furthermore, the reader can visualize, or relate to, the action, which leads to greater engagement in the content and better understanding of the ideas. Perhaps as importantly, action verbs reduce the chance that the reader will find your writing dull.

In contrast, state-of-being verbs provide very little content, if any, to a sentence. They communicate that something was, is, or will be something else, and they don't help the reader answer "Who did what to whom?" Overall, state-of-being verbs add padding to a document, and they result in dull writing.

To the extent possible, use action verbs. This won't be possible with every sentence, but when you use a state-of-being verb, consider how the sentence can be revised to use an action verb. Example C.6 shows how this is possible.

Example C.6a: "The purpose of this switch <u>is</u> to turn the power off." (State-of-being verb)
Example C.6b: "This switch <u>turns</u> the power off." (Action verb)

Example C.6a, with the state-of-being verb *is*, equates *the purpose of this switch* with *to turn the power off.* Example C.6b demonstrates direct writing. It uses the action verb *turns* and tells what the subject does. Additionally, example C.6b communicates concisely, which will typically occur when a writer uses action verbs.

Action verbs and nominalizations: Nominalizations are the noun forms of action verbs, as seen in Table 2.

Table 2: Sample Action Verbs and Corresponding Nouns (Nominalizations)

Sample action verbs	Corresponding nouns
illustrate	illustration
fail	failure
react	reaction
announce	announcement
increase (v.)	increase (n.)

Nominalizations have multiple negative effects.

1. They make sentences less concise.
2. They increase the noun-to-verb ratio.
3. They make sentences difficult to understand.
4. They make reading tedious.

Nominalizations often force writers to add additional words to sentences. Changing nominalizations back to action verbs often decreases the number of words needed to communicate the idea, as seen here:

> *Example C.8a, with nominalization:* "The <u>commencement</u> of the ceremony will be at noon."
> *Example C.8b, without nominalization:* "The ceremony <u>will commence</u> at noon."

> *Example C.9a, with nominalization:* "This example provides an <u>illustration</u> of the problems with nominalizations."
> *Example C.9b, without nominalization:* "This example <u>illustrates</u> problems with nominalizations."

The revised versions also have lower noun-to-verb ratios. In example C.8, the noun-to-verb ratio drops from 3:1 to 2:1. In example C.9, the noun-to-verb ratio drops from 4:1 to 3:1. As a result, the revised sentences state their message in clear, concise, and interesting language.

Nominalizations characterize *legalese, businessese, academese,* and all other -*ese* types of writing. They characterize writing that is difficult to understand and tedious to read. As the number of nominalizations increases, the reader's difficulty understanding also increases. Using action verbs solves these problems.

Table 3: Revising Sentences with Nominalizations and Lowering the Noun-to-Verb Ratio

	Original	Ratio		Revised	Ratio
1.	An <u>expansion</u> in the <u>utilization</u> of pencils was the <u>cause</u> of the <u>reduction</u> in the <u>utilization</u> of red ink. (19 words)	7:1	1.	People are using less red ink because they are using more pencils. (12 words)	2:1
2.	The <u>analysis</u> <u>process</u> that was the <u>requirement</u> of the <u>experimentation</u> protocol is an <u>indication</u> of researchers' <u>lack</u> of <u>ability</u> in data <u>synthesis</u>. (22 words)	5:1	2.	The way the researchers analyzed the data indicates they do not know how to synthesize data. (16 words)	1:1

Upon reading the original versions of the two sentences above, the reader may rightly ask, "What is the writer trying to say?" The sentences do not communicate well because they have too many nominalizations. They have other problems, too. Both sentences use state-of-being verbs as the main verbs and not the meaningful action, and neither sentence uses the meaningful subject. They also require many words to communicate the message.

The revised versions are far superior. First, and most importantly, they are easy to understand. Second, they answer "Who did what to whom?" Third, they are concise, with seven and six fewer words, respectively. Fourth, they use action verbs as the main verbs. Overall, the revised versions demonstrate direct writing.

(Notice also that when I revised the second example, I was able to remove *requirement of the experimentation protocol* because it became self-explanatory.)

Nominalizations are acceptable in two situations:

1. Providing common names, and
2. Ending main ideas.

First, nominalizations help communicate common titles and things.

Nominalizations like these do not make sentences difficult to understand, and they allow the writer to state ideas succinctly. For example, *consultant* is a noun form of the verb *consult*. However, *consultant* describes a common type of person or job, as in "The consultant advised us to sell our stocks." If you were to revise this sentence to avoid *consultant*, you would need many more words to express your idea.

As another example, *illustration* is a noun form of *illustrate*, but when used to describe a drawing or a picture, it is acceptable, as in "The illustration shows how the parts are assembled." If you were to replace *illustration* with *image*, for example, you would be replacing one noun for another, so the revision is no better than the original.

Second, nominalizations can provide a feeling of closure to a sentence.

One of the reasons nominalizations make reading tedious is they are "heavy" words. They force the reader to pause and consider the meaning, which quickly becomes mentally fatiguing. However, a nominalization at the end of the sentence gives the reader the sense that the idea is now complete. In very non-technical terms, they end a sentence with a "thud." In this way, they help a sentence have more impact on the reader. This can be useful at the end of a paragraph or at the end of an important point or main idea. In the two examples that follow, the second example provides greater impact.

Example C.10a, weak: "Fertilizer helps plants grow faster."
Example C.10b, strong: "Fertilizer accelerates growth."

Thus, a nominalization may be acceptable if it

1. makes the sentence more concise, or
2. accents your main idea.

In all other cases, and to the extent possible, avoid nominalizations. Your writing will be more concise, more understandable, and more direct.

D. Verb Voice

Active and Passive Voice: When you are active, you do something. When you are passive, things happen to you. This is the same concept as the active and passive voice in sentences.

In the active voice, the subject performs the action described by the main verb. In the passive voice, the action described by the main verb is done to the subject.

Example D.1a, active voice: "The service team collected the parts."
(subject: *service team*; main verb: *collected*)
Example D.1b, passive voice: "The parts were collected by the service team."
(subject: *parts*; main verb: *collected*)

In example D.1a, the subject did the action, so the sentence is active. In example D.1b, the action was done to the subject, so the sentence is passive. To determine whether your sentence is active or passive, first find the subject and main verb. Then ask, "Is the subject doing the verb?" If the answer is Yes, then the sentence is active. If the answer is No, the sentence is passive.

If we describe this concept as a formula, we get this:

S → V = active (the subject does the action)
V → S = passive (the action is done to the subject)

Grammatically, the active voice looks like this:

Subject – Verb – Object (i.e., *Who did what to whom?*).

On the other hand, the passive voice uses the object as the subject of the verb, resulting in

Subject/Object – Verb (i.e., *To whom was it done?*).

By using the object as the grammatical subject, a passive voice sentence makes the information convoluted and complex, and the reader will be less likely to respond to it. Additionally, the meaningful subject will never be the grammatical subject in the passive voice, which means the reader won't focus on the person or thing doing the action.

In nearly every sentence, the active voice results in more direct writing. However, the passive voice has a purpose, too. Next, we'll look at the reasons for each voice.

Reasons for active voice: The main reason for using the active voice is that it directly answers the readers' question, "Who did what to whom?" It provides the desired information and in that order. As a result, the reader can more easily understand and remember the idea you wish to communicate.

Other reasons include the following:

1. The active voice is more likely to use the meaningful subject as the grammatical subject and the meaningful action as the main verb.
2. Sentences in the active voice are more engaging because something is performing an action.
3. Active voice sentences are generally more concise.
4. The active voice emphasizes active verbs.

In brief, the active voice follows the principles of direct writing.

Reasons for passive voice: The passive voice may be appropriate for two reasons:

1. To de-emphasize the person or thing doing the action, and
2. To shorten the grammatical subject.

First, the main reason for using the passive voice is to hide or de-emphasize the meaningful subject. Instead, the passive voice emphasizes the person or thing on which the action was performed, as seen in D.2a and D.2b.

> *Example D.2a, passive, emphasizes the material:* "The material was first developed in the laboratory by researchers from Oslo."
> *Example D.2.b, active, emphasizes the researchers:* "Researchers from Oslo first developed the material in a laboratory."

In both D.2a and D.2b, the meaningful action is *developed*, making *researchers* the meaningful subject. Whereas the active voice sentence in D.2b uses the meaningful subject as the grammatical subject, the passive voice sentence in D.2a does not. If the writer wishes to focus on the material, and if the researchers are not important (or not at this point in the document), the writer might prefer the passive voice.

Scientific writing, regardless of the field, does not require the passive voice. This also applies to dissertation writing. The active voice is perfectly appropriate for describing the research methodology. The purpose of the research methodology is to describe what the researchers did to collect and analyze the data. Thus, the researchers are correct to use the active voice when describing their actions. Instead of writing

"The data were collected from six species of house sparrows,"

the researcher can write

"We collected data from six species of house sparrows."

However, in many cases, the writer can revise the sentence to use the active voice without mentioning the researchers, as seen here:

"Six species of house sparrows provided the initial data for analysis."

The second reason for using the passive voice is to simplify and shorten the subject of the sentence so that the main verb is closer to the beginning of the sentence and easier to find, as seen below.

Example D.3a, active voice sentence: "The decision whether to solicit for and hire a new personnel manager or to outsource those functions to an external agency consumed valuable work time." (subject: 21 words)

Example D.3b, passive voice sentence: "Valuable work time was consumed by the decision whether to solicit for and hire a new personnel manager or to outsource those functions to an external agency." (subject: 3 words)

If we remove all the descriptive words from example D.3a, it reads, "The decision consumed time." Example D.3a uses the meaningful subject *(The decision whether to . . .)* as the grammatical subject, and it focuses the readers' attention on the main idea of the sentence. For these reasons, example D.3a is more direct than example D.3b. However, the subject contains 21 words, greatly delaying the reader from reaching the main verb.

If we remove all the descriptive words from example D.3b, it reads, "Time was consumed by the decision" Example D.3b uses the object *(Valuable work time)* as the grammatical subject, forcing the meaningful subject to the end of the sentence. However, the grammatical subject contains only three words, so the reader can reach the main verb more quickly.

Examine every passive voice sentence carefully to make sure it is the better choice. Other than in these two cases, the active voice will generally produce better writing.

5. CONCISE WRITING

Concise writing is clear writing. By definition, concise writing communicates in as few words as necessary. This does not mean you should only use short sentences. The quality of a sentence is not determined by its length but by the value of the words it contains. Concise writing uses only necessary words. And then it stops.

Concise writing has two benefits:

1. It communicates clearly, and
2. It demonstrates respect for the reader.

The basic strategy for concise writing is (1) to determine what you want to communicate and then (2) to determine whether your sentences communicate that message as succinctly as possible. Look for words, phrases, and sentences that do not contribute to your message and either move them to where they are relevant or remove them completely.

This does not apply to literary writing wherein the "flavor and beauty" of the writing is part of the readers' enjoyment. It applies to technical and academic writing wherein your primary purpose is to communicate information.

The first, and most important, strategy for concise writing is to write directly—see Chapter 4.

Other basic strategies for writing concisely follow.

A. Combine Verbs and Action Objects

The direct object is the thing on which the action is performed. For example, in "We increased the brightness by a factor of 6," the action *increased* is performed on the thing *brightness*. Thus, *brightness* is the direct object. (The simple way to find the direct object: Say the verb and ask "What?" The answer will be the direct object, as in "increased what?" *Brightness*.)

A direct object that names an action is an *action object* (this is my term). You can often use an action object as the main verb, making the sentence more concise.

> *Example A.1a, not concise:* "The subjects <u>communicated their response</u> through an online survey."

In example A.1a, the main verb is *communicated*. The action object, *response*, names an action. We can use the action object as the verb and get example A.1b:

> *Example A.1b, concise:* "The subjects <u>responded</u> through an online survey."

Table 4 contains more examples showing various ways to apply this strategy.

Table 4. Combining Verbs and Action Objects

Original	Words	Revised	Words
1. The company <u>conducted</u> a full-scale <u>reorganization</u>.	6	1. The company fully <u>reorganized</u>.	4
2. Jim Thorpe <u>continued to play</u> football until age 41.	9	2. Jim Thorpe <u>played</u> football until age 41.	7
3. While <u>attempting to capture</u> images of ghosts, many paranormal research groups <u>rely on using</u> unscientific methods.	16	3. <u>To capture</u> images of ghosts, many paranormal research groups <u>use</u> unscientific methods.	12
4. The author <u>produced</u> clear <u>writing</u>.	5	4. The author <u>wrote</u> clearly.	4

B. Simplify Descriptions

Everything in a sentence other than the subject, verb, and object is description. Descriptions cause most of the "fluff" in sentences, but because they do not convey the main message, a careful writer can reduce them substantially without losing the main message. Strategies to simplify descriptions are below.

Simplifying ownership: You can show ownership in two ways, with a possessive or a prepositional phrase. Prepositional phrases always make writing less concise. Using possessives, such as the apostrophe-S, will make writing more concise.

> *Example B.1a, prepositional phrase:* "The <u>purpose of the CEO</u> is to create an environment for efficiency." (12 words)
> *Example B.1b, possessive:* "The <u>CEO's purpose</u> is to create an environment for efficiency." (10 words)

In example B.1, revising the prepositional phrase reduces the sentence's word count by two words. This might not seem significant, but it is. First, if you do this multiple times in a document, the overall effect is more concise writing. You will have removed many unnecessary words. Second, the writing will be stronger overall because you will have removed the weak prepositional phrases.

I only endorse prepositional phrases for ownership when the "owner" is a phrase of three or more words. With the possessive, the sentence may be confusing or awkward because the sentence has multiple descriptive words before naming the thing being described. Each case needs to be considered carefully. In example B.2, the sentence with the prepositional phrase may be better than the sentence with the possessive.

> *Example B.2a, prepositional phrase:* "The design of the ergonomic latex foam chair compensates for spine curvature."
>
> *Example B.2b, possessive:* "The ergonomic latex foam chair's design compensates for spine curvature."

However, when you have multiple owners, possessives are generally better. Example B.3 demonstrates this concept with mutual owners, and example B.4 demonstrates this concept with separate owners.

> *Example B.3a, prepositional phrase:* "The agreement between the owner and the buyer resolved the confusion." (11 words)
> *Example B.3b, possessive:* "The owner and buyer's agreement resolved the confusion." (8 words)

> *Example B.4a, prepositional phrase:* "The offices of the president and vice-president display the constitution." (11 words)
> *Example B.4b, possessive:* "The president's and vice-president's offices display the constitution." (9 words)

Simplifying adverbial phrases: Adverbial phrases describe how an action is performed. They answer the question "How" regarding the verb (e.g., Ran how? Worked how?). You may be able to replace the phrase with one or two words without changing the meaning. Although I generally don't recommend using adverbs, a single adverb is far superior to an adverbial phrase, as seen in example B.5.

> *Example B.5:* Wrote in a manner that used few words to convey the message → Wrote succinctly

In fact, this is one of the few cases in which I recommend using adverbs. Use this strategy only when you can't find a verb that explicitly describes the action and doesn't require a modifying adverb or adverbial phrase. If you can find an accurate verb that doesn't require modifiers, use it, as seen in Example B.6.

> *Example B.6:* Drove at a high rate of speed → Drove fast → Sped

Table 5 shows how single adverbs can replace adverbial phrases.

Table 5. Using Single Adverbs to Replace Adverbial Phrases

Verb + Adverbial phrase	Verb + Adverb
1. walked a few steps at a time	1. walked hesitantly
2. administered the survey as the initial step of the process	2. first administered the survey
3. removed the gray matter in a careful manner	3. removed the gray matter carefully

Simplifying adjectival phrases: Adjectival phrases describe what something is. Following the concept that using fewer words is better, concise writers reduce adjectival phrases to single words when possible. This is particularly important when a sentence has two or more phrases in a series. Consider example B.7a.

Example B.7a: "The finances of a hospital that provides free healthcare services to needy families and other financially challenged persons without insurance to cover the cost for services will always fluctuate." (29 words)

This sentence is a mess. The basic sentence is "The finances will fluctuate." Everything else is description and is fair game for revision. The entire phrase *that provides free healthcare . . . cover the cost for services* describes *hospital.* A name for such a hospital is *charity hospital.* Now we have this:

Example B.7b: "The finances of a charity hospital will always fluctuate." (9 words)

We might try "A charity hospital's finances will always fluctuate," but that sounds awkward to my ear. This revision may be more drastic than necessary, but the sentence has other opportunities for cutting down the description. *Free healthcare services* can become *free services* because *healthcare* is implied—it's a hospital. A single word for *financially challenged* is *poor,* and a single word for *without the insurance to cover the cost for services* is *under-insured.*

Identify the adjectival phrases in a sentence and determine whether you can eliminate them or, at least, reduce them to single words.

Reducing multi-layer descriptions: You described something in your sentence, but some part of that description may be unclear. So you described something in your first description. Now, you have a description of the description. This is a problem for conciseness because the second description doesn't add value to main message. After the initial description, the new descriptions are off topic, distracting the reader from the point you wish to make. We see this problem in example B.8a.

> *Example B.8a, multi-layer description:* "The data collected by researchers from the university best known for education programs, according to Educ. Weekly, show that teachers prevent abuse."

Figure 2 shows that example B.8a has four layers of description, with each layer on a separate line. Four layers of description is three layers too many.

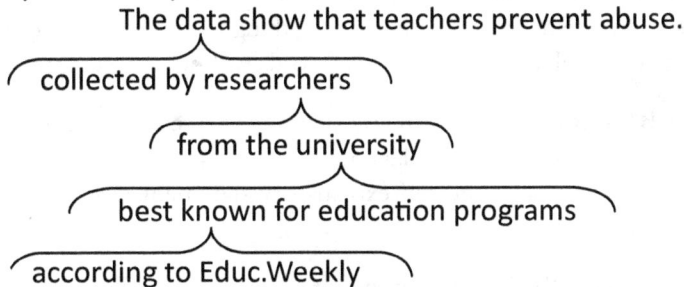

The data show that teachers prevent abuse.

collected by researchers

from the university

best known for education programs

according to Educ.Weekly

Figure 2. Multi-layered description.

The four layers of description in example B.8a are as follows.

- Initial word: *data*
- Layer 1: *collected by researchers* describes *data*
- Layer 2: *from the university* describes *researchers*
- Layer 3: *best known for education programs* describes *university*
- Layer 4: *according to Educ. Weekly* describes *known*

The strategy for reducing layers of description has two steps.

1. Determine whether all the descriptions are relevant. For example, in example B.8a, the university's reputation may

not be related to the data findings. Certainly, the journal name is not relevant here.

2. Move the description in layers 2+ to another sentence. If we decide that the reader needs to know about the university's programs, we can move that information to another sentence. It is off-topic here.

These two steps can lead to multiple revisions, including the following.

> *Example B.8b, single-layer description:* "According to Educ. Weekly, Blahblah University is best known for its education programs. Blahblah University researchers collected data on child abuse and found that teachers prevent abuse."

This sentence still has a problem with self-explanatory information, so we'll turn to that topic next.

Removing self-explanatory descriptions: If the description is (1) inherent in the context or (2) the definition of the thing being described, remove it. In short, remove anything to which the reader will respond, "Well, of course!" Those words will be unnecessary.

Example B.8b has this problem. By definition, researchers collect data. Someone who collects data is a researcher. With a slight revision, we can remove the self-explanatory statement *collected data* without losing meaning.

> *Example B.8c:* "Blahblah University researchers found that teachers prevent child abuse."

Let's look at the descriptive phrase "in the morning" and see how it is unnecessary in two cases.

> *Example B.9a, inherent in the context:* "Before the first daily milking in the morning, dairy cattle are more likely to demonstrate passive herd behavior."

The fact that this behavior occurs in the morning is obvious because the context is behavior prior to the first daily milking.

> *Example B.9b, part of the definition:* "Deliver the report by 10 a.m.

in the morning."

Based on the definition of *a.m.*, any action that occurs during a.m. hours occurs in the morning.

Removing self-explanatory descriptions requires critical thinking about what you write and why. The central question to ask is "Is this information already obvious?" If the answer is Yes, remove it.

Using positive statements: Negative statements tell the reader what something is not. They require the reader to understand a message and reverse it, causing more work than necessary and increasing the potential for misunderstanding. Negative statements tell the reader "I mean the opposite of this idea."

Negative statements commonly use such words as *not* and *no* and such prefixes as *un* and *non*.

Positive statements, on the other hand, tell the reader what something is, which is a central tenet of direct writing. A positive statement tells the reader, "This is what I mean." The following table provides examples of negative statements and possible revisions.

Table 6. Negative and Positive Statements

Negative statement example	Positive statement revision
1. Students cannot register through the website.	1. Students can register only in-person or by mail.
2. The CFO won't authorize purchases over $10K without full justification.	2. The CFO requires full justification for any purchases over $10K.
3. Energy costs are unaffordable.	3. Energy costs are too high.
4. A soda cannon is not a safe toy for small children.	4. A soda cannon is a dangerous toy for small children.
5. The recipe is incomplete.	5. The recipe is missing steps.

You probably will find cases where the negative statement is better than the positive statement. The negative statement may be better if

- the negative version is short and simple,
- the positive version takes many more words to express or is awkward, or
- the positive version is in the passive voice.

The negative statement in example B.10a may be better than the positive statement in example B.10b because the positive version is in the passive voice. However, example B.10c solves this problem.

> *Example B.10a, negative statement:* "This base solution contains an unknown quantity of mercury." (meaning: the quantity is not known)

> *Example B.10b, passive positive statement:* "The quantity of mercury in the base solution has yet to be determined."

> *Example B.10c, active positive statement:* "We do not know the quantity of mercury in the base solution."

If you wish to use a negative statement to emphasize some ideas, follow it immediately with the positive statement. This pairing of negative and positive statements is the "not this . . . but that" impact strategy, and it is effective. In all other cases, focus on positive statements.

The point is this: Positive statements are generally easier to understand and more direct. Use negative statements conscientiously and only when necessary.

C. Eliminate Redundancy

Provide your message clearly and once. Repeating yourself adds unnecessary words, thus diminishing reader interest, and gives the impression that you don't have anything else to say, thus diminishing your credibility. I have seen documents in which entire paragraphs are exactly repeated. This isn't redundancy; this is carelessness.

Redundancy comes in three forms:

1. Direct restatement (e.g., "as mentioned previously"),

2. Synonyms (e.g., "big and large" "concise and succinct"), and
3. Concept repetition

Direct restatements: You can remove direct restatements by strengthening the initial mention of the issue and then providing new ideas that relate to it. Using similar words can help the reader refer to the earlier information. If you didn't make the point clear the first time, repeating it won't help.

Synonyms: Don't use two words with similar meanings. Choose the most accurate word.

Concept revision: Concept repetition is the most difficult redundancy problem to solve because it requires critical thinking about the content. As you are writing, or reading, your ideas, ask yourself, "Have I already mentioned something like this?" If the answer is Yes, revisit the initial passage and determine whether you are providing new information or simply stating the previous information in a new way. Example C.1a provides two sentences that communicate the same concept.

> *Example C.1a:* "Teachers and students work together to develop learning expectations. Through their discussions, they determine what, and how much, the student should learn."

Both sentences in example C.1a describe the concept of teacher–student collaboration on learning goals. The first sentence seems more general and can be removed, which will require a slight revision to the second sentence. On the other hand, the two sentences can be combined, as seen in example C.1b

> *Example C.1.b:* "Teachers and students work together to determine what, and how much, the student should learn."

Removing concept repetition is more difficult when the redundant passages are widely separated. This becomes, then, an issue of organization as much as it is an issue of redundancy. With related topics close together and with ideas presented one at a time, redundant passages will be close together, making them easier to find and revise.

D. Remove Unnecessary Words

This strategy is a "catch-all" for any remaining issues with concise writing. Look at each word in your sentences and consider its importance. If it does not add any value, remove it. Table 7 has samples of words and phrases that may be safely removed in most cases without hindering reader understanding.

Table 7. Sample Unnecessary Words

Word/Phrase	Non-concise Sample	Concise Revision
a total of	A total of 7 people attended.	7 people attended.
all of the	All of the board members agreed.	The board members agreed.
really	The device really saves time.	The device saves time.
as you know	As you know, rotary engines are loud.	Rotary engines are loud.
very	Aspirin is very useful for relieving fevers. (This statement needs support. *Very* doesn't communicate anything by itself.)	Aspirin is useful for relieving fevers. (This statement also needs more support.)
along with	The senator, along with the governor, proposed new health legislation.	The senator and governor proposed new legislation.
that is / that are / that was	The delivery that is scheduled for tomorrow will be on time.	The delivery scheduled for tomorrow will be on time.

who is / who are / who was	A resident who is running for city office must file a petition.	A resident running for city office must file a petition.
now	The 3-cylindar engine is now obsolete.	The 3-cylindar engine is obsolete

In the same manner, many multi-word phrases can be reduced to one word, as seen in Table 8.

Table 8. Sample 1-Word Replacements for Multi-word Phrases

Multi-word phrase	1-word replacement
in spite of	despite
due to the fact that / in light of the fact that	because
at the present	now (remove this word, too, as seen in Table 7)
in regards to	regarding
at the current location	here
as soon as	when
more or less	approximately
in the vicinity of	near

E. Combine Related Sentences

If you have one sentence that explains a following or prior sentence, you may be able to combine the two sentences. This strategy is particularly useful when the explanatory sentence uses the same or similar words as in the main sentence. It prevents repetition and makes the writing more concise.

Combine the sentences by making the explanatory information a subordinate clause to the main point. A subordinate clause contains a subject and a verb and modifies the main clause (i.e., your main point). Example E.1 contains a subordinate clause, underlined.

Example E.1: "After the contractor completed the bridge repair, the city donated excess materials to Habitat for Humanity."

In example E.1, the main clause is *the city donated excess materials to Habitat for Humanity*. The underlined subordinate clause describes the main clause, in this case describing when the actions in the main clause occurred. Let's look at an example of this strategy.

Example E.2a: "Researchers finished mapping the gene group. Researchers used proprietary technologies to map the gene group."
Example E.2b: "Using proprietary technologies, researchers finished mapping the gene group."

Example E.2a has two sentences. The first sentence is the main point, and the second sentence describes the main point, stating how the researchers performed the task. The two sentences contain similar words. Example E.2b combines the two sentences by making the second sentence a subordinate clause of the first sentence. The subordinate clause precedes the main point, which keeps the main point as the final statement where it has more emphasis. These two sentences can be combined in other ways, too.

Example E.2c: "Researchers used proprietary technologies to finish mapping the gene group."

Example E.2c emphasizes using the technologies by making the main verb *used*. This is a problem because *using the technologies* is not part of the main point. Thus, example E.2b, using subordination, is the best choice.

My final advice for concise writing is this: Respect your reader and communicate effectively by saying only what needs to be said.

6. SENTENCE STRUCTURE

A. The Subject-Verb-Object Structure

Every sentence has two basic parts, the subject and verb. Many sentences contain a third basic part, the object. Together, these three parts contain the main message in a sentence, and they answer the readers' question: Who did what to whom? This means that they need to be as obvious as possible to the reader. Every sentence editing strategy springs from this concept.

Once you have identified the meaningful subject (section 4.A), meaningful action (section 4.B), and object, you can apply the S-V-O strategies below.

Place the verb as close to the subject as possible: The subject and verb are the two most important words in a sentence. When the verb immediately follows the subject, the reader will connect the verb to the subject and understand the main point of the sentence. In example A.1a, the verb is separated from the subject. In example A.1b, the main verb is next to the subject, and the sentence is easier to understand.

> *Example A.1a:* "Any checking account established by persons living outside the United States and not registered with the banking commission falls under international regulations."

In example A.1a, the subject and main verb are *account* and *falls*, respectively. 15 words of description separate the subject and verb, including three more verbs. This sentence has two potential problems. First, the separating words interrupt the main point of the sentence, which reduces the emphasis on the main point. Second, with three other verbs before the main verb, the reader may associate the wrong verb with the subject, causing the reader to misunderstand the main point entirely.

Examples A.1b and A.1c fix this problem by placing the main verb immediately after the subject.

Example A.1b: "Any checking <u>account falls</u> under international regulations if it is established by persons living outside the United States and not registered with the banking commission."

Example A.1c: "If a checking account is established by persons living outside the United States and is not registered with the banking commission, <u>it falls</u> under international regulations."

Place the main subject and verb at the beginning of the main sentence: Once the subject and main verb are together, move them to the beginning of the main sentence. This strategy is called "front loading" because it "loads" the beginning of the sentence with the most important information. By using this strategy, you immediately answer "Who did what to whom?" as seen in example A.2.

Example A.2: "<u>Submarine eruptions create new islands</u> through the gradual, though sometimes drastic, buildup of lava flows and other eruptive matter."

Even if the reader becomes confused with all the description, the reader will understand the main message. This strategy does not require every sentence to begin with the subject and verb, which would produce the "washboard effect" (section 6.B). Rather, it applies to the beginning of the main sentence.

Example A.3: "By using quantitative research methodologies, <u>researchers attempt</u> to identify common themes and patterns exhibited by the study population."

In example A.3, the sentence begins with a descriptive phrase. The main sentence begins with *researchers attempt,* which are the subject and verb. Indeed, readers expect to find the subject immediately after an introductory description. If the subject is not there, the sentence will seem awkward, and the reader may be confused.

Limit the number of subject–verb pairs: Every complete sentence has a main subject–verb pair. A simple sentence has one subject–verb pair, but a complex sentence may have several. Each additional subject–verb pair increases the level of complexity and increases the potential for confusion. Example A.4 has five subject–verb pairs.

> *Example A.4a:* "When <u>engineers envision</u> the required component <u>they will use</u> to perform a function, <u>they consider</u> how the <u>component fits</u> within a comprehensive system within which <u>components interact</u> and both enable and limit other components."

As the number of subject–verb pairs increases, the reader becomes more likely to identify the wrong pair as the main subject and verb. Limit the main sentence to no more than three pairs and any introduction to no more than one pair. Example A.4b follows this guideline.

> *Example A.4b:* "When <u>engineers envision</u> the component needed to perform a function, <u>they consider</u> how the <u>component will fit</u> within a comprehensive system. <u>They determine</u> how the various <u>components will interact</u> and how <u>they will enable and limit</u> other components."

This does not apply to subject–verb pairs within a series. The parallel structure of a series prevents reader confusion, as in example A.4c.

> *Example A.4c:* "When <u>engineers envision</u> the required component, <u>they consider</u> what function the <u>component will perform</u>, how the <u>component fits</u> within a comprehensive systems, and how the <u>components interact</u>."

Keep subject–verb pairs separate: As noted previously, a sentence may have more than one subject-verb pair. To improve the potential for reader understanding, keep the subject–verb pairs separate, i.e., finish one pair before introducing another.

Example A.5a has three subject–verb pairs but does not follow this strategy.

> *Example A.5a:* "The <u>business owners</u> *we serve* through a comprehensive set of tools our *experts created* <u>attain</u> greater financial stability."

In this sample, I underlined the main subject–verb pair and put the other two pairs in italics. The main subject in Example A.5a is *business owners*. However, before reaching the main verb, *attain*, the sentence has two more subject–verb pairs, *we serve* and *experts created*. Restructuring this sentence graphically helps demonstrate how two subject–verb pairs are embedded in the main pair.

The business owners
  we serve
    experts created
attain greater financial stability

Figure 3. Embedded subject–verb pairs.

To follow the one-at-a-time strategy, we can restructure the sentence as follows.

> *Example A.5b:* "Using a comprehensive set of tools our *experts created,* <u>we help</u> *business owners attain* greater financial stability."

Again, the main subject–verb pair is underlined and the other two pairs are italicized. Each pair ends before another begins. In this revision, the main subject–verb pair changes from *business owners attain* to *we help*, which makes us (or *we*) responsible for the result: *business owners attain greater financial stability*. If we want to keep the focus on the business owners (i.e., the meaningful subject), we use *business owners* as the grammatical subject. One possible revision is as follows.

> *Example A.5c:* "<u>Business owners attain</u> greater financial stability by using the comprehensive set of tools our *experts created.*"

Summary of S-V-O strategies: This section has provided a lot of information. In summary, these are the key strategies for using the basic Subject-Verb-Object sentence strategy.

1. Use the S-V-O sentence structure: meaningful subject + meaningful action + object.
2. Place the verb as close to the subject as possible.
3. Place the main subject and verb at the beginning of the main sentence.
4. Limit the number of subject–verb pairs.
5. Keep subject–verb pairs separate

When you follow these five strategies, you will solve most problems with sentence structure and reader understanding.

B. The Washboard Effect

The five strategies just presented will help you write clear sentences. However, if you are not careful, you may produce the *washboard effect*. The washboard effect describes the mental pattern created when every sentence begins with the subject and verb.

The reader pays greater attention to the subject of the sentence than to any other words. This creates a mental "bump" in the reader's attention. When these "bumps" occur repeatedly at the beginnings of sentences, they create a repetitive pattern, the mental equivalent to the sound of fingers running down a washboard. Figure 4 demonstrates this pattern.

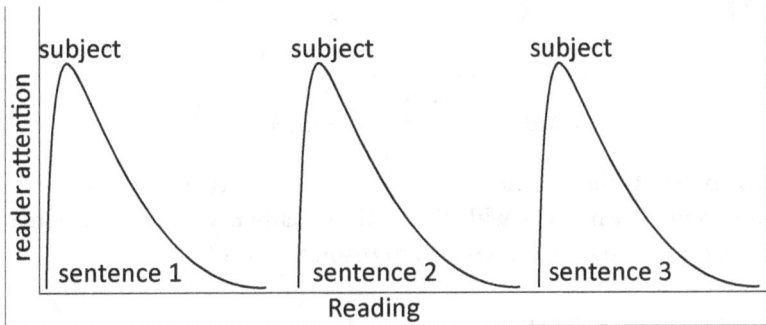

Figure 4. Washboard effect.

The paragraph in example B.1 demonstrates from the washboard effect. As you read it, you will recognize the pattern.

> *Example B.1:* "The automobile industry suffers from heavy labor demands. Labor demands have grown over the years. They now include extended time off with pay and greatly increased pension plans. The cost of supporting these labor demands is high. Manufacturers have had to reduce their profit margins to meet them. Lower profit margins cause slower or no growth. Automotive laborers are the ones who will suffer most. Fewer jobs will be available for new hires. Some current laborers will be retired or laid off. Manufacturers will

find robotic technologies to reduce the need for expensive workers."

Example B.1 follows the S-V-O strategies, but it is dull and difficult to read. Sentences that produce the washboard effect quickly become boring and tedious to read. And this is a problem if you want to interest the reader in your ideas. The reader will become disinterested and may soon forget the ideas you presented in prior sentences. As the pattern progresses, this is what happens to reader interest, with a bump for every subject:

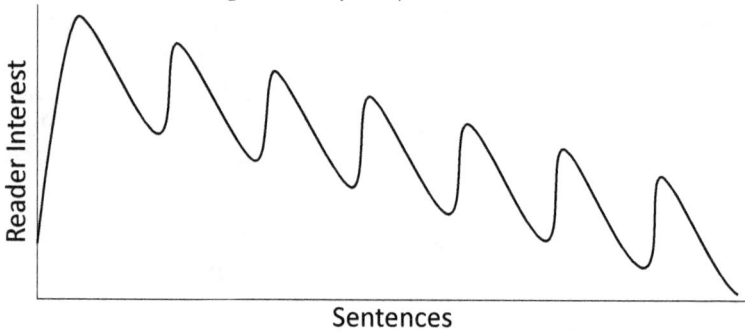

Figure 5. Washboard effect and reader interest.

To prevent the washboard effect, don't start more than two consecutive sentences with the subject. Rather, vary your sentence structures using the sentence patterns in Section C.

C. Sentence Patterns

A good writer needs only a few basic sentence patterns to follow the S-V-O strategies and avoid the washboard effect. All effective sentence patterns start with the S-V-O structure. Optional components are additional S-V-O structures and descriptive phrases and clauses, which can be placed in various locations.

Although each of these sentence patterns communicates clearly, do not use them with more than two consecutive sentences. Also, use the more complex sentence patterns less frequently. They are more challenging for the reader and may make the overall writing more complex than necessary.

In the samples below, the subjects are underlined, and the main verbs are italicized. In the formulas for each sentence pattern, *D* refers to a descriptive clause or phrase, *S* refers to the subject, *V* refers to the main verb, and *O* refers to the object of the verb.

Simple sentence (S-V-O): A simple sentence has one subject–verb pair and starts with the subject (or an adjective and the subject). The subject is immediately followed by the verb (or an adverb and the verb). Use no more than two consecutive simple sentences to avoid the washboard effect.

> *Example C.1:* "The computer <u>desktop</u> *provides* access to your files."

Simple sentence with a simple introductory description (D + S-V-O): The main sentence is a simple sentence. It is preceded by a simple descriptive phrase with only one level of description (C.2a) or a simple descriptive clause with only one subject and verb (C.2b). If you need to describe some aspect of the introductory description, use two sentences. Otherwise, the description will be overly complex and increase the potential for misunderstanding.

> *Example C.2a:* "As designed, the computer <u>desktop</u> *provides* access to your files."

> *Example C.2b:* "When your computer is working properly, the computer <u>desktop</u> *provides* access to your files."

Compound simple sentence (S-V-O + S-V-O): Two simple sentences are joined by a conjunction.

> *Example C.3:* "The computer <u>desktop</u> *provides* access to your files, and the external <u>hard drive</u> *stores* back-up files."

Compound simple sentence with a simple introductory description (D + S-V-O + S-V-O): This pattern combines the previous two patterns.

> *Example C.4:* "According to the user manual, the computer <u>desktop</u> *provides* access to your files, and the external <u>hard drive</u> *stores* back-up files."

Simple sentence with compound predicates (S-V-O + V-O): The subject has two main verbs.

> *Example C.5:* "The computer <u>desktop</u> *provides* access to your files and *contains* shortcuts to common programs and folders."

Simple sentences with compound objects (S-V-O + O): The verb has two objects. Not every sentence has an object, but sentences that can have one object can also have two objects.

> *Example C.6:* "The computer <u>desktop</u> *provides* access to your files and critical information about your computer."

Simple sentence with descriptive phrase for the subject or verb (S+D -V-O or S- V+D -O): A descriptive phrase follows the subject (C.7a) and either follows or precedes the verb (C.7b). If you use this pattern, keep the descriptive phrase as short as possible because it will separate the subject and the main verb or the verb from its object. A descriptive phrase does not have a subject and verb.

> *Example C.7a:* "The computer <u>desktop</u>, your starting point, *provides* access to your files."

> *Example C.7b:* "The computer <u>desktop</u> *provides*, as simply as possible, access to your files."

Simple sentence with ending descriptive phrase or clause (Sentence + D): Any of the previous sentence patterns can be followed by a descriptive phrase or clause. For example, the descriptive clause in example C.8a follows a simple sentence, the descriptive phrase in example C.8b follows a compound sentence, and the descriptive phrase in example C.8c follows a simple sentence with a simple introductory description.

> *Example C.8a:* "The computer <u>desktop</u> *provides* access to your files, which is handy when you need to locate a file quickly."

> *Example C.8b:* "The computer <u>desktop</u> *provides* access to your files, and the external <u>hard drive</u> *stores* back-up files, thus providing two ways to access all files."

Example C.8c: "As designed, the computer <u>desktop</u> *provides* access to your files, with back-up copies on the external drive."

Other sentence patterns: These eight sentence types will serve you well in nearly every instance. You can modify them to create other patterns. For example, you can add descriptive words in multiple locations. With each sentence you write, however, consider the level of complexity and consider whether a simpler pattern will work. Some cautions:

1. Keep the S-V-O pattern intact,
2. Only use one level of description, and
3. Use few descriptive clauses and phrases, if any.

D. Sentence Transitions

Sentences do two things:

1. Provide information to support the central idea of a paragraph, section, theme, etc.,
2. Create a logical flow of information.

Sections A through C have discussed strategies to communicate information within sentences, and Chapter 7 will discuss how sentences interact in paragraphs. Here, we will examine how to make a logical connection from the information in one sentence to the information in the next sentence. This is the purpose of sentence transitions.

Every sentence refers to the information in the previous sentence and adds new content. In other words, start with known information and finish with new information. Once written, new information becomes known information, which can be used to start the next sentence. This strategy connects information between sentences, as seen in Figure 6.

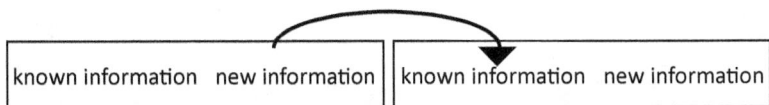

| known information   new information | known information   new information |

Figure 6. Sentence transition concept.

Example D.1 demonstrates how sentence transitions work. The beginning of sentence two will reflect the new information in sentence one, and the beginning of sentence three will reflect the new information in sentence two.

> *Example D.1:* "(1)The operant conditioning chamber was first developed by Skinner while he was a graduate student at Harvard University. (2)He used the chamber to study the effect of inputs on rats. (3)Various devices in the chamber provided inputs that, over time, 'taught' the rats to behave in predictable ways."

In example D.1, sentence two, the words *he* and *study* refer to the words *Skinner* and *student*, respectively, in sentence one. In sentence three, the words *chamber* and *inputs* refer to the words *chamber* and *inputs*, respectively, in sentence two. The sentences have other connections, too, but these examples demonstrate how the information in one sentence reflects the information in the previous sentence.

If you cannot make these transitions between sentences, you may need to revise, re-order, or remove sentences.

7. PARAGRAPH STRUCTURE

A. Paragraph Purpose

Whereas sentences communicate information about an idea, paragraphs communicate ideas. This is the most important concept to understand about paragraphs. Based on this concept, the purpose of a paragraph is to communicate information about one, and only one, idea.

One paragraph = One idea

Key strategy for writing paragraphs: The first strategy to writing an effective paragraph is to ask yourself, "What is the single idea I wish to discuss next?" Then, write a single paragraph about that idea.

Paragraphs do not have a recommended number of sentences. Rather, write as many, or as few, sentences as needed to communicate the idea. Long paragraphs are about big ideas; short paragraphs are about very specific, discrete ideas. To meet the principles of technical writing, I recommend discussing discrete ideas in short paragraphs. However, if you follow the strategies in this chapter, even long paragraphs with big ideas will be clear and easy to read.

Key strategy for editing paragraphs: The first strategy for editing a paragraph is to ask yourself, "What is the main idea being communicated in the paragraph?" With a well-written paragraph, you will be able to state the main idea in a single short sentence. On the other hand, if you determine that your paragraph communicates two ideas, find the sentence that begins discussing the new idea and split your paragraph into two paragraphs, each about one idea.

Once you have determined the one idea for a paragraph, examine your sentences. Because every paragraph communicates one idea, every sentence in the paragraph must communicate information about that idea. If you find a sentence not about the main idea, revise it or remove it.

B. The 3 Cs of Effective Paragraphs

Every well-written paragraph needs three parts: context, content, and conclusion. These three parts are known collectively as the 3 Cs. When you use the 3 Cs, you present information logically, you help the reader understand your message, and you demonstrate the relevance of your idea.

Context: The first sentence (or two) of a paragraph establishes the context. The context has two purposes:

1. Reveal the single idea that will be discussed, and
2. Demonstrate how the idea relates to the previously discussed idea.

To establish context, first determine the single idea you will discuss next. The first sentence (or two) presents that idea. Second, think about the logical connections between the idea and the previous idea. The first sentence (or two) provides the transition from one idea to the next by demonstrating those connections. Example B1 illustrates how context is established.

Example B.1:

"[final sentence of a paragraph about nurses' responsibilities]
When nurses fully understand these duties, they can interact as a team to improve patient well-being.
[first sentence, i.e., context, of the next paragraph] A patient may have many needs that a single nurse, or other healthcare provider, cannot address alone."

In example B.1, the first sentence of paragraph two establishes the context for the paragraph that follows. First, it reveals the main idea: patients have multiple needs. Second, it shows how the main idea connects to the previous idea. (Section C below will discuss these connections.) As a result, the reader will know what to expect from the paragraph, will be able to make sense of the information to follow, and will understand its relevance within the logical flow of ideas.

If you do not establish the context, the reader will have greater difficulty understanding your ideas. The reader may ask, rightly, "What am I reading about, and why?" The reader may be confused by the information, and you, as the writer, will seem to be presenting unconnected, irrelevant information that can be overlooked or forgotten. Without establishing the context, you increase reader confusion and reduce the level of communication.

Your job, therefore, is to ensure that each paragraph begins by establishing the context.

Content: Once you have introduced the idea and its relevance, you provide the content. The content is the information about idea, i.e., the body of the paragraph. Each sentence within the body supports the main idea, explains it, and helps the reader understand it. When the body of the paragraph is complete, the reader should have all the necessary information to understand the idea.

Example B.2 begins with the context (from example B.1, in italics) and provides information about the idea.

Example B.2:

"A patient may have many needs that a single nurse, or other healthcare provider, cannot address alone. For example, the patient may have diverse medical needs, such as examinations and treatments for a host of medical conditions. The patient may also have cultural needs based on the social norms, values, and perspectives of his or her community. Finally, a patient may have emotional needs resulting from the interaction of fear of death and hope for recovery."

Whereas the context in example B.2 introduced the idea that patients have multiple types of needs, the content described those needs. In this sample, the body of the paragraph listed three broad types of needs. Later paragraphs may discuss those needs in greater detail, which would make this entire paragraph the context for the document section.

Three details is not a "magic number." Provide as much, or as little, information as necessary to discuss the idea fully. Broader ideas require more information. Discrete ideas need less. The idea, therefore, determines the content—and the length of the body. If every sentence in the body helps the reader understand the idea, the body will be the right length.

Your job, therefore, is to provide the necessary information to understand the idea of the paragraph.

Conclusion: The conclusion is the final sentence (or two) of the paragraph, and it is the most difficult to write. Similar to the context, the conclusion has two purposes:

1.   Provide the conclusion, meaning, or purpose of the content, and
2.   Create a transition to the following paragraph.

Now that the reader has read the content, what do you want the reader to understand? What should the reader think about or do with the information? What action do you want the reader to perform? In short, what conclusion should the reader reach from the content you have provided? If you have done well with providing the content, the reader will be ready to accept your conclusion.

The second function of the conclusion is to create the transition to the next paragraph, which is exactly the same process as creating a transition with the context, though in reverse.

Example B.3 will conclude the paragraph example we're using to understand the 3 Cs.

Example B.3:

"*A patient may have many needs that a single nurse, or other healthcare provider, cannot address alone. For example, the patient may have diverse medical needs, such as examinations and treatments for a host of medical conditions. The patient may also have cultural needs based on the social norms, values, and perspectives of his or her community. Finally, a patient may have emotional needs resulting from the interaction of fear of death and hope for recovery.* To address this diversity of needs, a patient also needs a diverse team of caring, competent healthcare providers who work together to ensure the most positive outcome possible."

The final sentence in Example B.3 concludes the information about types of patient needs. It gives the meaning and value of the content to the reader and makes the argument that patients need multiple caregivers. The reader, having just read about the types of patient needs, will be ready to accept this conclusion. Your job, therefore, is to help the reader reach a conclusion and make sense of the content.

For every type of genre, but especially for academic and technical writing, 3 Cs structure not only works but also is necessary if your purpose is to present information clearly, logically, and purposefully.

C. Paragraph Transitions

Although each paragraph is about a unique idea, well-written paragraphs demonstrate how ideas connect. As noted previously, one function of the context is to demonstrate how the idea of one paragraph relates to the idea of the previous paragraph. Additionally, one function of the conclusion is to create a transition to the next idea. In brief, the last sentence of one paragraph needs to connect to the first sentence of the following paragraph. These connections create a logical flow of ideas.

To create these connections, or transitions, use the same words or phrases and refer to the same concepts in the final sentence of one paragraph and the first sentence of the next paragraph. This strategy causes the contents of the paragraph to overlap and shows how the ideas in the paragraphs connect. Figure 7 demonstrates how paragraphs overlap by using the same words, phrases, and concepts.

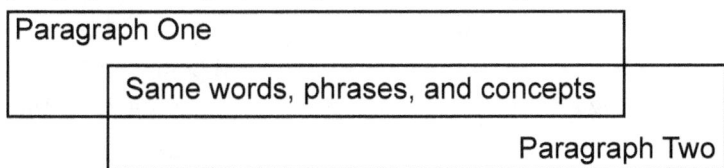

Figure 7. Overlapping paragraph content.

Example C.1 presents the final sentence of one paragraph and the first sentence of the following paragraph.

Example C.1:

". . . When nurses fully understand these duties, they can interact as a team to improve patient well-being.

A patient may have many needs that a single nurse, or other healthcare provider, cannot address alone . . . ."

In example C.1, the final sentence of paragraph one has at least four connections to the first sentence of paragraph two. *Duties* in paragraph one connects to *address* in paragraph two, *patient* connects to *patient*, *team (of nurses)* connects to *single nurse*, and *well-being* connects to *needs*. With four connections, the idea of paragraph two will seem like the logical extension of the idea presented in paragraph one.

When you edit your writing, look for these connections. If you only find one or two, you may need to revise your paragraphs. If you don't find any connections, you may need to revise the paragraphs or move entire paragraphs to create a more logical flow of ideas.

D. 1-Sentence Paragraph

A paragraph may have only one sentence. In journalistic writing, this is standard protocol. One fact, one paragraph. In most cases, this is not appropriate for technical writing, and it is never appropriate for academic writing.

Appropriate use: For technical writing, the one-sentence paragraph is appropriate when

- describing a list of steps,
- providing a series of bulleted or numbered points, or
- providing an impact statement or action step at the end of a discussion.

The first point refers to providing instructions, with each step in a process described by a single sentence. The second point refers to listing information in a bulleted list of complete sentences. These are visual tricks to help the reader locate and identify information.

The final point above is particularly challenging because it refers to using a one-sentence paragraph within a narrative text, i.e., as a paragraph within paragraph-based text. In this case, the one-sentence paragraph, too, follows the 3 Cs described previously.

When used appropriately, the reader already understands the context for the information in the sentence and already has the content for the topic of the sentence, based on information in the prior paragraph. And the prior paragraph must follow the 3 Cs. What the one-sentence paragraph does, therefore, is provide an impact statement, a key point that addresses the value, meaning, and purpose of preceding paragraphs. It provides a conclusion to the ideas presented across multiple paragraphs in a direct, simple statement.

When used appropriately, a one-sentence paragraph is a powerful tool to help your reader pay attention to and remember your most important points.

Inappropriate use: Although one-sentence paragraphs can indicate your most important points, they lose their impact when used frequently. Consider this: if you are indicating that many points are the *most important points*, then none of them are the most important; they are equally important. Each subsequent use reduces the impact of the sentence, eventually becoming distracting to the reader. Use one-sentence paragraphs infrequently, if at all.

8. SIGNPOSTS

Signposts in writing are much like direction signs on a road. They inform the reader how the information relates to prior information (i.e., where the reader was), what information is being presented now (i.e., where the reader is), and what information will be presented later (i.e., where the reader is going).

Signposts connect information across paragraphs, sections, and chapters. Long documents require signposts. Shorter documents, too, benefit from signposts. By including signposts in your writing, you increase reader understanding by helping the reader organize the information mentally.

Signposts come in four categories: outline indicators, point indicators, internal references, and headings.

Outline indicators: As indicated by the name, outline indicators reveal the outline for a document. They provide the order of the information. Outline indicators are also known as *sequence markers* because they indicate the sequence of the information.

Sample outline indicators: next, first, second, step one.

Point indicators: Point indicators inform the reader that you are about to communicate an important point. They increase reader attention and receptivity to the idea, fact, or piece of information you are about to provide.

Sample point indicators: now, at this point, finally, in conclusion, however

Internal references: This type of signpost refers to information you previously provided or to information you will provide later. You can use internal references to mention an idea that is more fully explained elsewhere in the document but that is also relevant to the current idea. By using internal references, you draw connections between major concepts in the document.

Sample internal references: as discussed in, later, furthermore, in a later chapter, as mentioned in

Headings: Headings are the most obvious type of signpost. Use them to label various sections and subsections in a document. They tell the reader exactly what you will discuss, and they create the table of contents for the entire document.

If possible, use no more than 3 or 4 heading levels. This book, for example, uses 3 levels of headings, and the table of contents includes only levels 1 and 2. If you use too many levels, you may confuse the reader. The reader uses headings to make a mental map of the information; if the map is too complicated, the reader may have difficulty remembering how the information connects.

SECTION C: WRITING MECHANICS

9. COMMAS

Commas are confusing because they are used in many ways. However, the basic principle to using commas is simple: Use commas to separate clauses and phrases within sentences that have their own meaning.

The "rules" for commas below are broadly, but not universally, accepted. However, a careful writer considers two central issues:

- Reader understanding and
- Consistency.

The comma guidelines below will help readers understand your message in many cases. However, even if they are not necessary to improve reader understanding, follow them for consistency. Consistency is a characteristic of academic and technical writing.

A. Series

The commas help the reader find each unique item (or group of items) in a series.

Example A.1: "School officials are dismayed by poor grades, low attendance, and high drug use."

B. Joining Sentences

You can join two complete sentences with coordinating conjunctions. (The entire set of coordinating conjunctions is *for, and, nor, but, or, yet,* and *so.* Together, these create the acronym *FANBOYS.*) The comma lets the reader know when one point is complete and the next will begin. This comma use only applies when you have complete sentences on either side of the conjunction.

Example B.1: "The screen inverter stopped working, <u>and</u> the motherboard began to smoke."

C. Introductory Descriptions

An introductory description is before the subject and describes the main verb in some way, such as when, where, how, and why. The comma at the end of the description signals the reader that the main point of the sentence is about to begin. For consistency, do this with even short introductory descriptions. In the following example, the introductory description is underlined.

> *Example C.1:* "Following the symposium, participants collaborated on projects."

D. Interjections

Technical writing is no place for interjections. However, if you use an interjection, separate it from the rest of the sentence with commas. In the following example, the interjection is underlined.

> *Example D.1:* "Hurrah, the project is finally complete."

E. Appositives

An appositive renames or restates the person or thing you just wrote. It is equal and indicates the identical information. Appositives are separated from the rest of the sentence with commas to indicate that the information is a restatement. In the following example, the appositive is underlined.

> *Example E.1:* "A *Do Not Resuscitate* order, a form of advanced directive, is often established during end-of-life care."

F. Asides, Interjected Comments, Parenthetical Expressions

While writing a sentence, you may want to include information that is not directly related to the main point of the sentence. To indicate that you are going "off topic," and to indicate when you are returning to the main topic, separate the information with commas. If you can put these expressions in parentheses, you can use commas, instead.

The information is not essential for understanding the point you are trying to make and, therefore, can be safely separated from the rest of the sentence.

> *Example F.1:* "The musical trends of the 20th Century, <u>as determined by a survey of published sheet music,</u> indicates a correlation between tempo and public confidence in the national economy."

G. Providing Examples

When you are providing examples of some fact or concept, you create a form of parenthetical expression. Thus, examples, too, are separated from the rest of the sentence with commas.

> *Example G.1:* "Alternative forms of transportation, <u>such as bicycles and roller skates,</u> are common but not popular in suburban areas."

H. Adjective Pairs

When you have two or more adjectives or other descriptions immediately before the word they describe, you may need to separate them with commas. If you can change their order, and if you can put *and* between them without changing the meaning of the sentence, the adjectives are called *coordinate adjectives* and need to be separated by a comma. The full explanation is far more technical, but if your adjectives meet these two conditions, you will place the commas correctly. The comma indicates that one adjective does not describe the following adjective in some way but that the adjectives equally describe the thing that follows both.

> *Example H.1:* "An <u>empowered,</u> <u>supported</u> student will find education exciting."

I. Non-restrictive Phrases and Clauses

A non-restrictive phrase or clause does not tell the reader which thing or person you are describing. Rather, a non-restrictive phrase or clause provides an "off-topic" description that is not necessary to understand the main point of the sentence. Separate all non-restrictive phrases and clauses from the rest of the sentence with commas. If the information is necessary for the reader to know which thing or person you are describing, do not use commas.

Example I.1: "The maple tree, <u>which harvesters tap for their sap to make syrup,</u> produces seeds in pairs."

Example I.2: "The CEO of Widgets.com, <u>who began his career as a shop clerk,</u> has a net worth of $1 million."

J. Dates

If you include the day, month, and year in the date, put commas around the year. If you do not include the day, you do not need the commas.

Example J.1: "On July 1, 2004, the publisher will release the new book series."

K. Final descriptive phrases and clauses

A sentence may end with a final descriptive phrase or clause. If the descriptive phrase or clause relates only to the words immediately prior to the description, you do not need a comma. However, if the description relates to the entire sentence, use a comma to separate it. This shows that the description relates to the entire sentence, not just one part of the sentence. (In the following example, the underlined description relates to the entire information in the main sentence. Without a comma, the sentence would indicate that *based on their website notice* describes why they postponed the ceremony.)

Example K.1: "The city council postponed the ceremony, <u>based on their website notice.</u>"

L. Quoted Text

In U.S. English, the final comma or period goes inside the ending quotation mark—even if it looks awkward or is not part of the quoted material.

> *Example L.1:* "According to business researchers, election results have a 'noticeable effect on stock prices,' and the entire stock market generally 'finds a new balance.' "

M. Conjunctive Adverbs

Conjunctive adverbs show how the idea in one statement relates to or modifies the idea in the prior statement. Table 9 lists common conjunctive adverbs

Table 9. Common Conjunctive Adverbs

additionally	likewise
certainly	nonetheless
however	rather
in contrast	therefore

Conjunctive adverbs are followed by a comma. In the next example, the conjunctive adverb indicates that the idea in the second sentence relates to or modifies the idea in the first sentence.

> *Example M.1:* "Academic learning increases employment opportunities. <u>However,</u> some higher education degrees provide greater opportunities than others."

N. Incorrect Comma Placement

Do not use commas in the following places within sentences.

1. Before *or* (in *either...or* expressions), *nor* (in *neither...nor* expressions), *but also* (in *not only...but also* expressions), or before the second part of similar two-part expressions.

   > *Example N1:* "The launch will occur <u>either</u> on Friday [no comma] <u>or</u> on Saturday."

2. Between the subject and predicate, unless the subject ends with an expression that requires commas, such as an

appositive.

> *Example N2:* "A substitute for natural wood products shipped from Finland [no comma] expands the market base."

3. Between two parts of a compound predicate.

    > *Example N3:* "Sound waves can produce heart palpitations in people within the wave cone [no comma] and can create pressure on sinus tissues."

4. Between two objects of a verb.

    > *Example N4:* "We use ocean currents to create electricity [no comma] and air currents to generate electromagnetic fields."

10. COLONS, SEMICOLONS, DASHES, AND HYPHENS

A. Colons

The purpose of the colon is (a) to end an independent clause and (b) to link something to the independent clause. For all practical purposes, an independent clause is a complete sentence. It can "stand alone" as a sentence. If the first part of the sentence is not an independent clause, you can't use a colon.

The colon has three purposes.

1. Introduce a list.

> *Example A.1:* "Consumers are interested in rayon materials for several reasons: low price, plentiful supply, and attractive appearance."

In example A.1, the colon ends the independent clause *Consumers are interested in rayon materials for several reasons* and introduces the list *low price, plentiful supply, and attractive appearance.*

Example A.1 demonstrates the list in sentence format. The punctuation remains the same if you write the list as a numbered or bulleted list, as seen in example A.2.

> *Example A.2:*
>
> "Consumers are interested in rayon materials for several reasons:
>
> * low price,
> * plentiful supply, and
> * attractive appearance."

The introductory statement in example A.2 is still an independent clause, so the colon is appropriate. Notice, also, that the commas and period remain the same whether the list is written in sentence format or bulleted format.

2. Link two independent clauses.

> *Example A.3:* "The plentiful supply of rayon affects consumers' interest in rayon: the large supply keeps the price low."

In example A.3, the colon links the first independent clause, *The plentiful supply of rayon affects consumers' interest in rayon*, with the second independent clause, *the large supply keeps the price low*.

3. Link a descriptive phrase to an independent clause.

> *Example A.4:* "Consumers' response to the price of rayon materials is predictable: more sales."

In example A.4, the colon links the descriptive phrase *more sales* to the independent clause *Consumers' response to the price of rayon materials is predictable*.

B. Semicolons

Colons have two purposes.

1. Link two independent clauses without a conjunction.

> *Example B.1a:* "The budget narrative includes the formulas for calculating costs; every cost item needs to be addressed."

The semicolon in example B.1 is linking two independent clauses without a conjunction. If the example had used a conjunction, it would need a comma instead of the semicolon, as in example B.1b.

> *Example B.1b:* "The budget narrative includes the formulas for calculating costs, and every cost item needs to be included."

The semicolon is only correct if the sentence parts before and after the semicolon are independent clauses. The only exception is when punctuating series, as in example B.2.

2. Separate items in a list when any of the items have their own commas.

> *Example B.2:* "The budget narrative provides costs formulas;

explains the needs for budget items, which should correspond to the program narrative; and summarizes costs by category."

Example B.2 has three items in a series. Normally, they would be separated by commas, but the second item has its own comma to separate the non-restrictive phrase *which should correspond to the program narrative.* To help the reader identify the items accurately, the items are separated by semicolons.

C. Dashes

Dashes come in two types: en dashes and em dashes. The en dash is the middle length one and is so named because it is about the width of the letter *N*. The em dash is the longest one and is so named because it is about the width of the letter *M*.

Table 10. Hyphen, En Dash, and Em Dash

hyphen	-
en dash	–
em dash	—

En dash: The en dash has two purposes.

1. Demonstrate a range (e.g., range of miles, range of years, range of ages).

> *Example C.1:* "Miles 12–64 will be under construction May–August."

2. Link two terms to describe a third term when the first term doesn't describe the second term.

> *Example C.2:* "The Bush–Kennedy education bill, known as *No Child Left Behind,* has been the subject of much controversy."

In example, C.2, *Bush* and *Kennedy* together describe *education bill,* but *Bush* does not describe *Kennedy.*

Notice that no spaces are around the en dash.

Em dash: The em dash also has two purposes.

1. Signal an off-topic statement within a sentence.

> *Example C.3:* "Our modern equipment—hand tools are out of date—operates at a high speed."

You can use parentheses instead of em dashes for this type of use. Interjecting off-topic statements in your sentence interrupts the point you are trying to make, so I do not recommend this use. If the information is necessary, place it in the prior or following sentence.

2. Add an emphatic statement to the end of a sentence.

> *Example C.4:* "Our equipment operates at a higher rate of speed than any comparable equipment in the industry—super fast."

Because this usage places heavy emphasis on the final statement, (a) keep the final statement short, (b) use this technique sparingly.

Notice that no spaces are around the em dash.

D. Hyphens

The hyphen has four purposes.

1. Link two words to describe a third word when the first word also describes the second word. This is the most common use of the hyphen.

> *Example D.1:* "We established a two-hour time limit for the examination."

In example D.1, the words *two* and *hour* are linked to describe *time limit*. Also, *two* describes *hour*, telling how many hours. Both conditions are met, so the expression *two-hour* requires the hyphen.

Many previously hyphenated expressions have become common terms and have either lost the hyphen or have been joined into single words. In most cases, however, this hyphen use is accurate.

If the descriptive expression follows the word it describes, it doesn't need a hyphen, as seen in examples D.2a and D.2b.

> *Example D.2a:* "The orchestra played Sibelius's well-known composition of music."

> *Example D.2b:* "The composition by Sibelius is well known."

Finally, if the first descriptive term ends in –ly, don't use a hyphen, as shown in example D.3.

> *Example D.3:* "These exceptionally preserved stamps are worth $1.2 million."

2. Add a prefix to a name.

> *Example D.4:* "The anti-Wilson campaign reduced voter attendance on election day."

3. Separate a prefix and word when the prefix ends with the same letter with which the word begins (optional).

> *Example D.5a:* "Students demonstrated improved achievement on the algebra post-test."

Using the hyphen in this way may also require you to use hyphens in other words for the sake of consistency, as seen with the term *pre-test* in Example D.5b.

> *Example D.5b:* "Students demonstrated improved achievement, based on their pre-test and post-test scores."

This hyphen use is not universally accepted. For example, some people write *posttest* and not *post-test*. The best advice is to be consistent and to follow most-common usage for particular terms.

4. Indicate a root word when adding the prefix creates a different word.

> *Example D.6a:* "The property owners will re-lease the house in August."

> *Example D.6b:* "The property owners will release the house in

August."

Adding a prefix to a word may result in writing what seems to be a completely different word. A hyphen can help the reader identify the base word and the prefix, leading to the correct interpretation. In example D.6a, the base word is *lease*, and the prefix is *re-*, indicating the owners will lease the house again. This sentence has a different meaning than the sentence in example D.6b. In example D.6b, the word *release* means to *let go*, indicating the property owners will give up or sell the house.

11. QUOTATION MARKS AND ITALICS

This chapter deals with 3 common questions:

1. Do I need quotation marks when paraphrasing?
2. Do I use quotation marks or italics when referring to specific terms or words?
3. If I use quotation marks, where does the final punctuation go?

A. Quoting vs. Paraphrasing

One principle of technical writing is to give credit to your information sources. Tell the reader where you got your ideas, information, and facts. If you do not state that your ideas come from some source, you are, in fact, claiming that you are their author. Thus, you need to clarify which ideas are yours and which are from someone else.

Use quotation marks when using another author's words exactly. The quotation marks indicate that the other author, not you, wrote the words. Examples A.1a and A.1b demonstrate exact quotations with integrated and separate citations, respectively.

Example A.1a, integrated: "As Johnson (2012) stated, 'Students' behavioral histories determine the teachers' levels of intervention.' "

Example A.1b, separate: " 'Students' behavioral histories determine the teachers' levels of intervention' (Johnson, 2012)."

Don't use quotation marks when you are paraphrasing another author's words. Examples A.1c and A.1d paraphrase the author's words using integrated and separate citations, respectively.

Example A.1c, integrated: "Johnson (2012) explained that the history of a student's behavior determines what interventions the teachers use."

Example A.1d, separate: "The history of a student's behavior determines what interventions the teachers use (Johnson, 2012)."

Whether you are quoting or paraphrasing, cite the author.

B. Punctuation with Quotation Marks

This section refers to the punctuation at the end of text within quotation marks. These guidelines reflect U.S. English conventions. For British English conventions, see below.

Commas and periods: Commas and periods go inside the final quotation mark. Example B.1 demonstrates this with a comma, and example B.2 demonstrates this with a period.

> *Example B.1, comma:* "The president declared March 5 a national holiday for honoring writers 'who seek to expand our children's minds through the power of language,' and the Senate passed the proclamation."

> *Example B.2, period:* "Wilson described the Rocky Mountains as a place where 'the lands of heaven meet the face of God.' "

Colons, semicolons, and dashes: Colons, semicolons, and dashes go outside the final quotation mark, unless they are a part of the quoted text.

> *Example B.3, colon:* "Wall Street financiers asked for one 'unanticipated and non-negotiable promise': protection against lawsuits from corporate bondholders."

Question marks: Question marks go inside the final quotation mark if the quoted text is a question, as in example B.4a. Otherwise, they go outside the final quotation mark, as in example B.4b.

> *Example B.4a, inside question mark:* "The county commissioner asked the NOAA spokesperson, 'Will the floodwaters recede prior to the next hurricane?' "

> *Example B.4b, outside question mark:* "Will the floodwaters recede before the next 'damn blaster comes through'?"

C. Italics and Quotation Marks to Refer to Words

When writing about words and phrases, as opposed to using them in a sentence, you have two options: put them in quotation marks or put them in italics.

I strongly recommend putting them in italics. If you put them in quotation marks, you may indicate that you are quoting another person or source. However, by putting them in italics, you indicate only that you are writing about words and phrases. Example C.1 demonstrates this use of italics.

Example C.1: "Find the outlet marked *Stereo* below the power button."

On the other hand, if you use a word in an unusual way, or if you wish to imply a meaning different than a word's connotative meaning, put it in quotation marks. This provides a clue that the reader should not interpret the word by its normal meaning, as demonstrated in example C.2.

Example C.2: "The memo expressed the 'friendly' message that the company would be disbanded."

12. GRAMMAR

A. Subject–Verb Number Agreement

The basics of subject–verb agreement: The number of the subject determines the number of the verb. If the subject is plural, the verb must be appropriate for plural subjects. If the subject is singular, the verb must be appropriate for singular subjects. Table 11 lists sample singular and plural subjects.

Table 11: Sample Singular and Plural Subjects

Singular	Plural
cat	cats
I	we
John	John and Bob
flower	flowers

Subject–Verb agreement causes problems only in the present tense. Unlike verbs in other tenses (e.g., past tense, future tense), present tense verbs change according to whether the subject is singular or plural.

Table 12: Subject and Verb Agreement, by Person and Number

	Singular	Plural
First person: (refers to the writer)	I eat	We eat
Second person: (refers to the reader)	You eat	You (all) eat
Third person: (refers to someone else)	**He, She, It, Who** eats	They eat

In the third-person singular, the present tense verb has an "S." Thus, if the subject of a verb can be replaced by *he*, *she*, *it*, or *who*, the present tense verb has an "S." Remember: "S" for "Singular."

Once you determine the subject for a verb, decide whether the subject refers to a single person or thing or to more than one person or thing. Examples A.1a and A.1b have singular and plural subjects, respectively. The subjects are underlined, and the verbs are italicized.

Example A.1a, singular subject: "The principal investigator *leads* the research team."

Example A.1b, plural subject: "The principal investigator and finance director *lead* the team."

Subject–verb agreement with "to be" verbs: In the present tense, "to be" verbs include the following.

Table 13: Subject–Verb Agreement with "To Be" Verbs

	Singular	Plural
First person: (refers to the writer)	I am	We are
Second person: (refers to the reader)	You are	You (all) are
Third person: (refers to someone else)	**He, She, It, Who** <u>is</u>	They are

As seen in Table 13, third person, if you can replace the subject with *he*, *she*, *it*, or *who* (singular subject), use *is* for the verb. If you can replace the subject with *they* (plural subject), use *are* for the verb. Again, remember: "S" for "Singular."

Subject–verb agreement with and *and* or: The word *and* will indicate a plural subject, and the verb will also be plural. In example A.2a, *and* indicates that the subject includes more than one person, i.e., is plural.

Example A.2a: "The principal investigator **and** the finance director *lead* the team."

The word *or* will indicate a singular subject if both parts of the subject are singular, and the verb will also be singular. In example A.2.b, the subject is either one principal investigator (single person) or one finance director (single person).

> *Example A.2b:* "The principal investigator **or** the finance director *leads* the team."

However, if the subject includes *or* and either part of the subject is plural, the verb will be plural. In example A.2c, one part of the subject is *research directors*, which is plural.

> *Example A.2c:* "The principal investigator **or** the research directors *lead* the team."

Subject–verb agreement with either: When the subject includes *either*, the verb may be singular or plural. If *either* refers to a pair of people or things, the verb will be singular. In this case, *either* indicates *either one*. In example A.3a, *either* refers to a pair of children.

> *Example A.3a, pair:* "If either of the children *has* symptoms, bring him to the clinic."

If *either* is followed by *or*, use the same guidelines as for *or*. If both parts are singular, use a singular verb, as in example A.3b. If either of the two parts is plural, use a plural verb, as in example A.3c.

> *Example A.3a, singular* either/or: "Either the older or middle child *is* likely to display symptoms."

> *Example A.3b, plural* either/or: "Either the older child or both younger children *are* likely to display symptoms."

Subject–verb agreement with any and all: The word *any* may have a singular or plural verb. If *any* refers to *any one*, the verb will be singular, as in example A.4a. If *any* refers to more than one, the verb will be plural, as in example A.4b.

> *Example A.4a, singular* any: "If any flight *lands* on time, notify the people on the waiting list."

Example A.4b, plural any: "If <u>any</u> flights *land* on time, notify the people on the waiting list."

The word *all* follows the same guidelines as *any*. If *all* refers to a singular noun, the verb will be singular, as in example A.5a. If *all* refers to a plural noun, the verb will be plural, as in example A.5b.

Example A.5a, singular all: "<u>All</u> the <u>salt</u> *dissolves* in the solution."

Example A.5b, plural all: "<u>All</u> the salt <u>crystals</u> *dissolve* in the solution."

***Subject–verb agreement with* every, everyone, *and* everything:** *Every, everyone,* and *everything* are singular words. Although they may refer to many people or things, these words refer to them all at once, as if they were one thing As such, these words require singular verbs, as in example A.6.

Example A.6: "Prior to opening the business, ensure that <u>everyone</u> *understands* his or her duties."

B. Pronoun–Antecedent Number Agreement

The basics of pronoun–antecedent agreement: Similar to subjects and verbs, the number of the antecedent determines the number of the pronoun. (The antecedent is the word to which the pronoun refers.) A singular antecedent requires a singular pronoun, and a plural antecedent requires a plural pronoun. Figure 7 helps clarify the term *antecedent* and demonstrates pronoun–antecedent agreement.

Each year, graduate <u>students</u>, armed with <u>their</u> new diplomas, seek jobs.

        plural antecedent   **plural pronoun**

Figure 8. Antecedent–pronoun agreement.

As seen in Figure 8, the antecedent *students* is plural, i.e., refers to more than one person. The pronoun *their* refers to *students* and is also plural. Thus, the antecedent and pronoun agree. Table 14 below provides samples of singular and plural pronouns.

Table 14. Sample Singular and Plural Pronouns

Singular	Plural
I, me, my	we, us, our
you, your	you
he, his, she, her, its	they, them, their
everyone	

Examples B.1a and B.1b show incorrect and correct agreement, respectively.

> *Example B.1a, incorrect agreement:* "Every dog owner finds something to love about their pet."
> *Example B.1b, correct agreement:* "Every dog owner finds something to love about his or her pet."

We can parse example B.1a to understand why it is incorrect. The pronoun *their* refers to the antecedent *every dog owner*. *Their* is a plural pronoun; it refers to more than one person. However, the antecedent to *their* is *every dog owner*, which is singular. A singular antecedent has a plural pronoun, meaning the pronoun and antecedent disagree.

To confirm that *every dog owner* is singular, we see that it is the subject to the verb *finds*, which is also singular. Thus, the incorrect example has a singular subject / antecedent, a singular verb, and a plural pronoun. Example B.1b corrects this problem by using the singular pronouns *his* and *her*.

C. Solving the Singular "They"

The term *singular "they"* means using the plural pronouns *they, their,* and *them* as singular pronouns referring to singular antecedents. Example B.1a above uses the *singular they*, and the discussion that follows explains why this is wrong. But it is very common.

Writers use *they* (and related pronouns) to refer to singular antecedents for 3 reasons:

1. They either don't know how to use correct grammar or they hear and read this mistake so often that it seems correct;

2. They wish to avoid gender-specific pronouns, such as *he* or *she*, when describing people of both genders; and
3. They understand why the *singular they* is wrong, but they don't know how to fix this error.

Three strategies will solve this mistake.

Use singular pronouns: The easiest solution is to change the incorrect plural pronoun for singular pronouns. The pronouns *he*, *his*, and *him* are all correct, though many people will consider these pronouns to be sexist, believing that they only refer to male people. Instead, you can use such expressions as *his or hers*, *he or she*, and *him or her*. Example B.1b above uses this solution.

Although this solution works, it can make writing tedious and cumbersome when used frequently. The next two solutions are better in most cases.

Use plural antecedents: If you want to use a plural pronoun, make the antecedent plural, as in example C.1. This is the most common, and easiest, solution to the *singular "they."*

> *Example C.1a, incorrect agreement:* "Any employee who arrives late will have their lunch privileges suspended."
> *Example C.1b, plural antecedents:* "Employees who arrive late will have their lunch privileges suspended."

Example C.1b has the plural antecedent *Employees* and the plural pronoun *their*. The antecedent and pronoun agree. Notice, also, that the verb changed from the singular *arrives* to the plural *arrive*.

Avoid the pronoun: In some cases, you can simply remove the pronoun and revise the sentence if needed. Examples C.2 shows how this works.

> *Example C.2, no pronoun:* "Any employee who arrives late will have lunch privileges suspended."

D. Subject vs. Object Pronouns

Subject pronouns: Pronouns that can serve as the subjects of verbs are called *subject pronouns*. Table 15 shows the only choices for subject pronouns.

Table 15: Subject Pronouns

	Singular	**Plural**
First person: (refers to the writer)	I	We
Second person: (refers to the reader)	You	You (all)
Third person: (refers to someone else)	He, She, It, Who	They, Who

Examples D.1a and D.1b show incorrect and correct pronoun use for the subject of a verb.

> *Example D.1a, incorrect pronoun:* "The patent holder and <u>me</u> *initiated* a new contract agreement."
> *Example D.1b, correct pronoun:* "The patent holder and <u>I</u> *initiated* a new contract agreement."

In example D.1a, the pronoun *me* is serving as the subject to the verb *initiated*. However, *me* is not a subject pronoun. Example D.1b corrects this error by using the subject pronoun *I*.

This error is most common with compound subjects, i.e., the subject has two or more parts. By removing all parts of the subject except the pronoun, you can easily identify the incorrect and correct pronouns. For example, "Me initiated..." is wrong, and "I initiated..." is correct. Then, when you re-add the other parts of the subject, you will have "The patent holder and I initiated...," which is correct.

Object pronouns: Pronouns that can serve as the objects of verbs or the objects of prepositions are called *object pronouns*. Table 16 shows the only choices for object pronouns.

Table 16: Object Pronouns

	Singular	Plural
First person: (refers to the writer)	Me	Us
Second person: (refers to the reader)	You	You (all)
Third person: (refers to someone else)	Him, Her, It, Whom	Them, Whom

Examples D.2a and D.2b show incorrect and correct pronoun use for the object of a verb.

> *Example D.2a, incorrect pronoun:* "Therapy services *provide* <u>we</u> with a sense of hope."
>
> *Example D.2b, correct pronoun:* "Therapy services *provide* <u>us</u> with a sense of hope."

In examples D.2a and D.2b, the action *provide* is done to the object of the verb, and the pronoun serving as the object of the verb must be an object pronoun. Example D.2a uses a subject pronoun, *we*, which is incorrect. Example D.2b uses an object pronoun, *us*, which is correct.

We can apply this same concept to the pronouns *who* and *whom*.

> *Example D.3a, incorrect pronoun:* "The supervisor can *fire* <u>who</u> he wishes to fire."
>
> *Example D.3b, correct pronoun:* "The supervisor can *fire* <u>whom</u> he wishes to fire."

In examples D.3a and D.3b, the action *fire* is done to the object of the verb, and the pronoun serving as the object of the verb must be an object pronoun. Example D.3a uses a subject pronoun, *who*, which is incorrect. Example D.2b uses an object pronoun, *whom*, which is correct.

When we rephrase a sentence as a question, the same principle applies.

> *Example D.4a, incorrect pronoun:* "Who can the supervisor *fire?*"
> *Example D.4b, correct pronoun:* "Whom can the supervisor *fire?*"

In examples D.4a and D.4b, the pronoun in question is still the object of the action *fire*. Thus, the object pronoun *whom* is still correct. In these 2 examples, *whom* is not the subject of the verb *can*, even though the pronoun is immediately before the main verb. Rather, *supervisor* is the subject.

Thus far, we have discussed pronouns serving as objects of verbs. Pronouns serving as objects of prepositions follow the same guidelines, as in example D.5.

> Example D.5: "Fifteen cars will follow *behind* us."

To find the object of the preposition, first find the preposition. In example D.5, the preposition is *behind*. Next, ask "behind what?" or "behind whom?" The answer will be the object of the preposition. In example D.5, the object of the preposition is *us*, an object pronoun.

Elliptical sentences. An elliptical sentence is a sentence with implied words or words left out that are part of the meaning. Example D.6 is an elliptical sentence.

> *Example D.6:* "The CFO prefers low-cost solutions."

The implied words in example D.6 are "to higher-cost solutions," which would be written at the end of the sentence if they were included.

The concept of elliptical sentences affects pronoun choice. Consider the difference between the elliptical sentences in examples D.7a and D.7b.

> *Example D.7a, incorrect:* "Wilson has a better sales record than her."
> *Example D.7b, correct:* "Wilson has a better sales record than

she."

The implied word in example D.7a and D.7b is *does*, as in "Wilson has a better sales record than her/she does." The pronoun serves as the subject of the implied word *does*. Thus, the sentences needs the subject pronoun *she* to be correct.

In some cases, you can change the meaning of a sentence by choosing a subject or object pronoun, as in examples D.8a and D.8b. Implied words are in parentheses.

> *Example D.8a, subject pronoun:* "The clients send more e-mails to me than <u>she</u> (sends e-mails to me)."
> *Example D.8b, object pronoun:* "The clients send more e-mails to me than (they send to) <u>her</u>."

Here's the point: When choosing between object and subject pronouns, consider what words are implied, if any.

13. WORD USAGE

Accurate word usage leads to accurate reader understanding. Writers generally have two types of word usage problems: (a) using a word that does not mean what the writer intends, which may cause the reader to misunderstand or may cause the writer to lose credibility, and (b) using a word that has multiple meanings, which may confuse the reader or may lead to misinterpretation. If you are unsure how a word is used or what it means, either get help or find a different word.

Table 17, which begins on the next page, presents words I have frequently found misused, or used ambiguously, in technical and academic writing. They are presented as pairs of words inappropriately interchanged.

Table 17. Misused Word Pairs

That	*Which*
Use: The word *that* introduces a description to identify the thing about which the writer is writing. *That* introduces information necessary to understand the writer's information.	Use: The word *which* introduces a supplemental description of some known thing. The description is not necessary to differentiate among similar items or to understand the writer's meaning.
Example: "The 485-GT is the part <u>that</u> connects the steel rod to the motor."	Example: "Restaurants are beginning to offer buffalo steaks, <u>which</u> are higher in protein content than regular beef."
Discussion: Of all the parts, only one part connects the steel rod to the motor. *That* introduces information indicating the part to which the writer is referring. "Of all the parts," the writer is saying, "I mean *that* part."	Discussion: The reader knows what type of meat the writer is discussing: buffalo meat. *Which* introduces a supplemental description of buffalo meat. If the writer removes the description, the reader will still understand the writer's main idea.
That begins a restrictive clause, meaning it restricts the reader's attention from a group of similar things to a single thing.	*Which* begins a non-restrictive clause. It doesn't restrict attention to a single thing because the thing being discussed is already known.

Who, restrictive	*Who, non-restrictive*
Use: Use *who*, not *that*, to indicate which person you are describing. The restrictive *who* has the same purpose as *that*, but for people. It is not preceded by a comma.	Use: Use *who*, not *which*, to provide a supplemental description about a person. The non-restrictive *who* has the same purpose as *which*, but for people. It is preceded by a comma.
Example: "The Speaker of the House is a congressman <u>who</u> leads the majority party."	Example: "Voters continue supporting their congressman, <u>who</u> has served for 12 years."
Discussion: The description beginning with *who* indicates which congressman is being described and is, therefore, essential information	Discussion: The description beginning with *who* is not essential to indicate which person is being discussed.
Like	*Such as*
Use: The word *like* indicates similarities. "A" is like "B," meaning "A" is similar to "B" and that "A" and "B" are different things.	Use: The expression *such as* introduces examples or a sample list.
Example: "American football, <u>like</u> Australian rugby, can be a violent contact sport."	Example: "Some sports, <u>such as</u> American football and Australian rugby, are violent contact sports."
Discussion: The word *like* indicates football and rugby are similar. They are not the same thing, but they have something in common.	Discussion: Football and rugby are examples of violent contact sports; however, they are not the complete list of violent contact sports.

I.E.	**E.G.**
Use: This expression, the initials for *id est*, indicates that whatever follows *i.e.* defines or means the same as whatever precedes *i.e.*, that one thing is the same as another thing.	Use: This expression, the initials for *exempli gratia*, indicates that whatever follows *e.g.* is a sample of whatever precedes *e.g.* E.G. introduces examples and is synonymous with *such as*.
Example: "Some sports, <u>i.e.</u>, American football and Australian rugby, are violent contact sports."	Example: "Some sports, <u>e.g.</u>, American football and Australian rugby, are violent contact sports."
Discussion: *I.E.* indicates that *some sports* means American football and Australian rugby. According to this statement, the only violent contact sports are football and rugby.	Discussion: *E.G.* indicates that football and rugby are examples of *some sports*, not the complete definition.

Effect	**Affect**
Use: In most common use, *effect* is synonymous with *result* or *resulting change in conditions*. *Effect* is a noun.	Use: In most common use, *affect* is synonymous with *alter* or *influence*. *Affect* is a verb.
Example: "The funding produces the desired <u>effect</u>."	Example: "The new funding <u>affected</u> our forecast."
Discussion: The funding produced some change in conditions or produced a result.	Discussion: The funding altered, or influenced, the forecast.
Note: *Effect* is used infrequently as a verb meaning *to cause to happen*.	Note: *Affect* is used as a noun only when describing a person's emotional conditions: a person's affect is the expression of his or her emotional state.

Compose	*Comprise*
Use: To make up or be a part of something greater.	Use: To gather, collect, or assemble parts as part of a whole thing.
Example: "Six boxes <u>composed</u> the entire delivery."	Example: "The delivery <u>comprised</u> six boxes."
Discussion: This word is often used in the passive voice, as in "The entire delivery was composed of 6 boxes." Here, the focus is on the parts and how they make something else.	Discussion: Here, the focus is on the whole thing and how it aggregates parts, as one thing comprises, or assembles, multiple parts into a whole.
Note: Many people would use "was comprised of" in the discussion example, but they would be wrong.	
Less	*Fewer*
Use: A lower quantity of a single, non-countable thing or mass noun.	Use: A lower number of individual things.
Example: "My car has less gas than yours."	Example: "We have fewer eggs today than yesterday."
Discussion: Mass nouns and non-countable things are sometimes hard to identify, but generally, they are single substances that comprise multiple parts, such as how a quantity of sugar contains multiple sugar grains and how time contains multiple hours, minutes, seconds, etc.	Discussion: If you can count them individually, use *fewer*.

Good	*Well*
Use: *Good* is an adjective. It describes the quality of people, places, things, and ideas.	Use: *Well* is an adverb. It describes actions, adjectives, and other adverbs.
Example: "This is a <u>good</u> plan."	Example: "Plants breed <u>well</u> under these conditions."
Discussion: I have never heard anyone use *well* in place of *good*. *Good* describes nouns and only nouns. If you are not describing a noun, don't use *good*; use *well*.	Discussion: *Good* is frequently used to describe actions, but this usage is incorrect. Unless you are describing a noun, use *well*.
If	*Whether*
Use: In standard, technical use, *if* provides a condition for something to occur.	Use: In standard, technical use, *whether* introduces options.
Example: "<u>If</u> the computers arrive tomorrow, we will start work."	Example: "Work will begin <u>whether</u> (or not) the computers arrive tomorrow."
Discussion: *If* is sometimes used to introduce options, as in "Work will begin if the computers are here or not." This is substandard and imprecise usage.	Discussion: Often, the alternative option isn't stated, though it's implied. Regardless, when you are describing options and possibilities, use *whether*.

Lay	Lie
Use: *Lay* most commonly means to put or place something. Alhtough this word has other meanings and connotations, we will discuss only this particular usage.	Use: *Lie* means to be in a horizontal position on top of something else. (It also means to knowingly make a false statement, but that's a different, less confused, form of *lie*.)
Discussion: *Lay* is a transitive verb, meaning an action that is performed on something else.	Discussion: *Lie* is not transitive, meaning it is not performed on something else.
Present tense example (lay): "I <u>lay</u> the book on the table."	Present tense samples (lie): "I <u>lie</u> in the bed."
Past tense samples (laid): "I <u>laid</u> the book on the table."	Past tense samples (lay): "I <u>lay</u> in the bed."
Present participle samples (laying, requires a *to be* verb): "I <u>am laying</u> the book on the table."	Present participle samples (lying, requires a *to be* verb): "I <u>was lying</u> in the bed."
Past participle samples (laid, requires a *to have* verb): "I <u>have laid</u> the books on the table."	Past participle samples (lain, requires a *to have* verb): "I <u>had lain</u> in the bed."

Since	**Because**
Use: *Since* means "from the time of."	Use: *Because* means, roughly, "as caused by" or "for the following reason."
Example: "I have been ill <u>since</u> eating the eggplant."	Example: "I have been ill <u>because</u> I ate the eggplant."
Discussion: This word can mean either "because" or "from the time of." To improve accuracy and clarity, use it only in the sense of "from the time of," leaving *because* to mean "because."	Discussion: Many people will use *since* to mean *because*. However, *because* has only one meaning, so using *because*, not *since*, to refer to causes will improve clarity.
Staff	**Staff member**
Use: *Staff* means a group of people who perform specific tasks within an organization.	Use: People on a staff are *staff members*.
Example: "The <u>staff</u> is expected to arrive early."	Example: "Three <u>staff members</u> are late."
Discussion: *Staff* is a singular noun. It refers to the people as a group. An approximate synonym is *team*, which is used in the same manner. The plural of *staff* is *staffs*.	Discussion: *Staff member* is singular; *staff members* is plural. When referring to individual people, or people within a staff, use *staff members*. An approximate synonym is *team members*, which is used in the same manner.

Data (singular)	**Data** (plural)
Use: Don't use *data* as a singular. This is sub-standard usage.	Use: All the pieces of data within a set. This is standard usage.
Incorrect example: "The <u>data</u> shows a strong positive skew."	Example: "The <u>data</u> show a strong positive skew."
Discussion: Many people, and some reference books, claim *data* can be used as a singular. It can, but it is substandard because it affects clarity, reducing the differentiation between the entire set of data points and individual data points. In casual writing, you may not be criticised for using *data* as a singular (e.g., "the data is"), but technical and academic writing have a higher standard. For a single piece of data, or some pieces of data within a set, use *piece of data, pieces of data,* or *data points.*	Discussion: Note that *show* is plural, unlike *shows*, which is singular. With *data*, you refer to all the individual pieces of data; you are writing about all of *them.* Thus, the verb needs to be plural. If you use a pronoun to refer to the data, you also need a plural pronoun, such as *they.* Use *data* the same way you use *facts* (plural).

14. TECHNICAL LANGUAGE USE

A. Jargon and Slang

Slang: Slang is colloquial language use. It consists of non-standard terms and expressions used by a specific social group in informal settings. The meanings of slang words and expressions are generally different than the dictionary definitions. All euphemisms, for example, are slang.

Slang is never appropriate in academic and technical writing. It is not formal language, and it may be misunderstood by readers outside the social group that uses it.

Jargon: Jargon consists of words and expressions common to a particular field of study or occupation. Jargon terms and expressions may be uncommon to, or used differently by, the general population. Unlike slang, jargon may be acceptable in academic and technical writing.

The following table provides example of jargon and the field in which they are used.

Table 18. Sample Jargon and Associated Fields

Jargon	Field
individualized	education
morgue	journalism
code 8	law enforcement
left / right	politics
register	linguistics
bear market	finances
cookie	computer technology

Jargon is only acceptable when a document is

- written for a narrowly defined reader population that understands and commonly uses the jargon, or
- written about a particular field of study or occupational field.

Jargon serves a communication purpose when writing about a particular field or occupation. Thus, when writing to readers who commonly use the jargon, use the jargon. Anything else will either seem condescending to the readers or will be inappropriate. Chapter 3, section A discussed *professional* language use; jargon is acceptable and common in that language style.

However, if you are writing to a general reader population, or if you are unsure whether the readers will understand the term, either avoid the jargon or define it at first use.

B. Acronyms

Acronyms are words and terms formed from the initial letter or letters of a name or expression. Examples include *SES* (socio-economic status, pronounced as individual letters), *MADD* (Mothers Against Drunk Driving, pronounced as a single word), and *Interpol* (International Criminal Police Organization, pronounced as a single word).

Acronyms are acceptable in academic and technical writing. Indeed, they prevent writers from using long, cumbersome terms and titles repeatedly, which would otherwise make the writing dull. Some acronyms have become common terms used and understood by the general population, such as scuba (self-contained underwater breathing apparatus) and laser (light amplification by stimulated emission of radiation). Such acronyms may be used freely without explanation because they are common terms. As an indicator of their normal use, these acronyms are not capitalized.

On the other hand, most acronyms can be defined multiple ways. For example, *NATO* can be either the North Atlantic Treaty Organization or the National Association of Theatre Owners. Others are specific to particular fields, similar to jargon.

Use acronyms as you would use jargon. At the first use define them, as seen in example B.1.

> *Example B.1:* "Shareholders may find their Individual
> Retirement Accounts (IRS) balances reduced."

Notice in example B.1 that the complete term is first spelled out in long form and then the acronym is provided in parentheses. Once you have defined the acronym, you can use it without re-defining it.

When you are writing to a narrowly defined audience that commonly uses a particular acronym, you may not need to define the acronym. For example, if I am writing a letter to an agent at the Internal Revenue Service, I will use the acronym *IRS* without first defining it. However, because acronyms may have multiple meanings, define them at first use when you are not sure whether the readers will understand them or when writing to a general audience. Acronyms are a form of jargon, and the principles for using acronyms are identical to the principles for using jargon.

C. This, That, and Other Vague Pronouns

This, that, these, those, and similar words can be used as either a pronoun or an adjective. When used as pronouns, they cause much confusion, forcing the reader to ask "This what," "That what," etc. Example C.1 demonstrates how these words can confuse the reader.

> *Example C.1a:* "Nutrition monitoring is effective when accurately performed with fidelity. That requires participants to keep ongoing food intake logs."

In example C.1, *that* is a pronoun that could refer to either *nutrition monitoring* or *performed with fidelity*. This example demonstrates the problem with this type of vague pronoun. The words *any, each,* and *all* have the same problem.

To prevent potential confusion, use these words not as pronouns but as adjectives. Answer the question "This what?" etc. You will be adding an additional word to the sentence, but you will also be reducing the potential for confusion. When we apply this strategy to example C.1a, we remove any doubt as to what *that* means, as follows.

> *Example C.1b:* "Nutrition monitoring is effective when accurately performed with fidelity. That monitoring requires participants to keep ongoing food intake logs."

In example C.1b, *that* is an adjective to describe, or identify, *monitoring*. Can you use such words as *this* as pronouns? Yes, but do so carefully, ensuring that they can only refer to one thing. The safe practice is to use them only as adjectives.

D. Writing numbers

No universally accepted rules address whether to use numerals or words for numbers. Indeed, the only agreed-upon concept is to select a style and follow it consistently.

If you are required to follow a particular style guide (e.g., APA, MLA, AP), follow the guidelines for that style. On the other hand, if you are not required to follow a particular style guide, you can pretty much do what makes sense to you and, most importantly, what will most help the reader to understand. Just be consistent.

I have my own guidelines that seem to work well in most cases. They are as follows.

1. Use numerals for numbers that need three words, words for numbers that need fewer than three words.

    Example D.1: "ninety-nine" "one hundred" "101" "two hundred" "6,201"

2. Use numerals for all numbers in document sections with many numbers being compared or discussed, as in this section.

3. Use words for any numbers that start a sentence.

    Example D.2: "One hundred and one dogs escaped from the kennels."

4. Use numerals for all numbered items.

SECTION D:
TECHNICAL
AND ACADEMIC
DOCUMENTS

15 DOCUMENT STRUCTURE

Central principles to document structure:

- The structure needs to help the reader find, understand, and use the content;
- The structure must be logical; and
- The structure needs to support, not detract from, the content.

With these principles in mind, we will examine various elements of document structure.

A. Principles of Document Organization

Whole document level: Documents, like paragraphs, have three components: Context, Content, and Conclusion, i.e., the 3 Cs. Regardless of how many sections a document has or how many topics it covers, it needs these three parts.

For example, a dissertation generally has 5 chapters. Chapter 1 provides the context: a broad overview of the topic, its importance, and the need for study. Chapters 2 through 4 are content: specific information about the issue from the research literature, methodology for studying the issue, and findings from the study. Chapter 5 is the conclusion, covering such issues as next steps for research and implications.

As another example, a "how-to" manual for small engine has the same components, too. It may begin with an overview of the process, the engine assembly, and situations in which repair is needed. This is context for what follows. Then, the manual may discuss various repair techniques. The conclusion may address actions to take if the repair was not successful or places to get further support.

As a final example, consider proposals for grant funding. The first section, the context, describes the need for funding, the current conditions, and why they are a problem. The second section, the content, describes what you propose to do about the current conditions. The final section, generally, is budget and evaluation plan.

The 3 Cs are important at the whole-document level.

- Context: A person reading the document needs to know what he will find inside, whether or not it's important to him, and background information to understand the contents.
- Content: Assuming the reader believes the document has value, he wants the information.
- Conclusion: Now that the reader has the information, the content, what actions should follow?

The context may be the most challenging section to write. You have to persuade your reader to keep reading, to care about the content, and to understand its relevance. The context, therefore, is persuasive writing.

Section or chapter level: Document sections and chapters, too, follow the 3 Cs—and for the same reasons. You first answer, "What's in this section and why is it relevant?" You then provide the details and information about the central topic of the section or chapter. You conclude with next steps or the central point you wish to make.

The structure of the entire document, therefore, looks like this, with as many or few sections as needed:

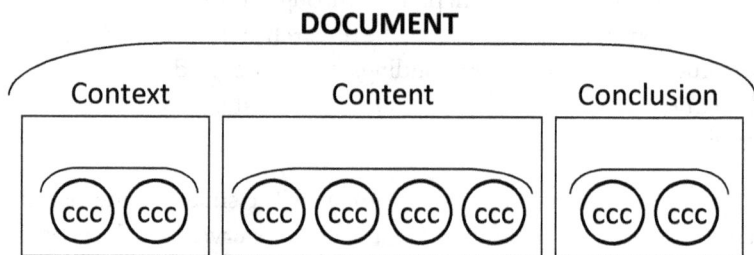

DOCUMENT

Context	Content	Conclusion
CCC CCC	CCC CCC CCC CCC	CCC CCC

Figure 9. Document structure.

B. Document Components

A document may contain many components. Common components are listed below in the order that they commonly appear. Select the components that will be useful to the readers or that are required by publishers, professors, or style requirements. Add others as needed.

1. Cover
2. Organizational Content
   a. Copyright information
   b. Synopsis / executive summary
   c. Table of contents with at least two levels of headings.
   d. Table of tables
   e. Table of figures
3. Topical Content
   a. Introduction
   b. Section or chapter title page
   c. Section or chapter content
   d. Conclusion
4. Supplementary Content
   a. Endnotes
   b. Citations / References / Bibliography
   c. Appendices
   d. Index
   e. Additional Resources

C. Headings

Headings do two things for readers:

1. Help locate information
2. Demonstrate how specific content relates to larger topics

As such, headings must be obvious and logical. On the other hand, a common trap is to use too many headings or too many levels of headings. Readers can become easily confused by multiple levels of headings. I generally try to keep to 3 levels, though sometimes (rarely) I need 4 levels.

To determine how many are appropriate in your document, consider the readers' needs, how the reader will use the document, and how you have organized the information into topics and subtopics.

Heading styles: If you are required to follow a particular style guide (e.g., APA, MLA, AP), follow the guidelines for that style. On the other hand, if you are not required to follow a particular style guide, you can pretty much do what makes sense to you and, most importantly, what will most help the reader to understand.

Heading styles follow one general principle: Heading importance determines the degree to which the heading is noticeable on the page. I have my own guidelines that seem to work well for most technical and academic writing. They are as follows.

Heading one: Center justified, bold, title case, 12 point, Times New Roman, paragraph by itself

This Is a Heading One

Heading two: Left justified, bold, title case, 12 point, Times New Roman, paragraph by itself

This Is a Heading Two

Heading three: Left justified, bold, paragraph case, 12 point, Times New Roman, followed by colon or period (If you do not have space between paragraphs but are using first-line indents instead, indent this heading, too.)

This is a heading three: (The text continues on)

Heading four: Left justified, italics, paragraph case, 12 point, Times New Roman, followed by a colon or period (If you do not have space between paragraphs but are using first-line indents instead, indent this heading, too.)

This is a heading four: (The text continues on)

You will notice that I do not follow these guidelines exactly for this book, although I do follow the general principle. This is not an academic text or article submitted for publication. In many cases, the final published texts, books particularly, have a more "stylistic" heading style. The purpose, however, is the same: help the reader find information and understand how content is organized.

Seriation: Seriation refers to numbered lists, whether they are presented in sentence format or as a series of items on subsequent lines of text. If a series has more than 3 items, use individual lines. The specific items in the series will be far easier to identify and understand.

Following are the three most common forms of numbered lists for technical and academic writing. In each case, punctuate the numbered lists as if they were written out in sentence format.

Example C.1a, Series that continues a sentence:

"Qualitative methodologies provides multiple advantages, including

1. Rich data for analysis,
2. Ability to explore unexpected concepts, and
3. Meaningful interpretation from the participants' perspective."

In example C.1a, the numbered items are required to complete the sentence, meaning they are necessary for the sentence to be grammatically correct. You could not put a period after *including*. As such, the introductory statement is not followed by a period, colon, or dash. Also notice that each numbered item is followed by a comma and that the second to last item is followed by *and*.

Example C.1b, Lists following an independent clause:

"Qualitative methodologies provides multiple advantages:

1. Rich data for analysis,
2. Ability to explore unexpected concepts, (and)
3. Meaningful interpretation from the participants' perspective."

In example C.1b, the introductory statement is an independent clause; it could serve as a complete sentence. As such, the statement is followed by a colon. Also notice that each numbered item is followed by a comma. The *and* after the second to last item is optional.

Example C.1c, Stand alone sentence list items:

"Qualitative methodologies provides multiple advantages.

1. They provide rich data for analysis.
2. They enable the researcher to explore unexpected concepts.
3. They explore interpretations from the participants' perspective."

In example C.1c, each listed item is a complete sentence. The introductory statement and items are punctuated using standard sentence punctuation.

Bullets vs. Numbered Lists: Numbered lists suggest an order to, or priority among, the items. The first item, therefore, is either the first in a list of steps or is more important than the following items. If this is not your intention, use a bulleted list instead.

16. ATTRIBUTION

A. Key Principle

One principle of technical and academic writing is to credit the sources of information. This includes both direct quotations and paraphrased information. Directly quoting means using exact words, figures, and images from a published source. Paraphrasing means restating information in your own words, which includes recreating tables and figures.

In short, if something is not your idea or writing, don't claim that it is: tell the reader where the information originated. Otherwise, you are guilty of plagiarizing. In academic writing, plagiarism may lead to a failing grade or expulsion from the academic program. In technical writing, plagiarism may lead to rejection of the document or a lawsuit. It's that serious. Don't do it.

B. Basic Information for Attribution

The key to avoiding plagiarism is to provide the reader with sufficient information to identify the source of the information. At a minimum, include the following:

- Author or organization that published the original information,
- Title of the original publication,
- Year of publication, and
- Publisher name.

In many cases, you may need to include the Internet address (i.e., URL), as well.

Various style guides (e.g., APA, MLA, Chicago, AP) provide specific directions regarding what information to include, the order to include it, and the format. If you are required to follow a specific style guide, do so. Otherwise, select a format and follow it consistently.

(My personal favorite, which I use when the style is not specified, is the APA style.)

C. In-text citations, Footnotes, and Endnotes

Immediately following the quoted material, provide the reader with necessary information to identify the source. Either use an in-text citation that refers to a reference list entry or use a reference number that directs the reader to a footnote or endnote.

If you use an in-text citation, include a reference list at the end of the document. The in-text citation should provide sufficient information for the reader to find the correct entry in a reference list. Typically, in-text citations provide the last name of the original author and the publication year.

If you use a reference number, the number should refer to the bibliographic description of the source document, whether you use endnotes or footnotes. Superscript the reference number, like this:[1]. (Most word processors will do this automatically.) Typically, the reference number comes before the period that ends a sentence, but this is not universally accepted. Choose a method and be consistent.

For most academic documents, use in-text citations and a reference list. For most technical documents, use a reference number with endnotes or footnotes. Generally, footnotes are used for providing supplemental information about content on the same page, and reference lists and endnotes are used for bibliographic information.

17. TABLE FORMATTING

Tables are excellent for presenting numbers and text for comparison. Use them to help the reader identify, separate, and understand specific information. Tables can also be overly complicated and ugly, diminishing both reader understanding and document professionalism.

As with many other issues, specific style guides may have unique specifications for the table format. Here are my recommendations for creating tables that not only look good but also enhance understanding.

1. Add a table number and title above the table.
2. Add a solid line above and below the entire table.
3. Add a line between a column title and the information that follows.
4. Add as few lines between table cells as necessary to visually separate the information.
5. Don't use a table when a bulleted or numbered list is sufficient.

The following table exemplifies these recommendations.

Table 19. Sample Table to Demonstrate Table Format Recommendations

Format	Required	Not Required
Using two lines for table number and title		X
Numbering the table	X	
Adding a table title	X	
Placing the table title above the table		X
Using bold or italics for table title and number		X

Capitalizing major words in the title		X
Double-spacing content in tables		X
Adding column headings for details	X	
Centering text in table cells		X
Adding lines on the right and left sides of the table		X
Adding lines between all rows or columns		X

Regarding capitalization, centering, bolding, and other non-required elements, choose a format and be consistent, only doing what is necessary to improve reader understanding and interpretation. Overall, think carefully about the table structure and format, asking what the reader needs and how the reader may interpret the information.

Of course, if you are required to use a specific style (e.g., APA, MLA), follow the guidelines of that style.

One last recommendation: Learn to use the table features on your word processor. Using those features is far superior to using the space bar or tab key to create tables and will save you much time and anguish.

18. STYLES AND STYLE SHEETS

As discussed here, style refers to the appearance of the text. It includes font selection, heading format, indentation, margins, justification, and many similar issues. If you are required to follow a specific style guide (e.g., APA, AP) or publisher style, those choices have been made for you. Otherwise, you can do pretty much what you want as long as you are consistent.

A. Text Style Recommendations

As with all writing concepts, consider your readers' needs. My recommendations follow.

- Font selection: Use Times New Roman or other standard serif font for the main text. (Serif fonts have little "feet" at the bottom of the letters. Serifs help the readers' eyes track straight across the line.) Avoid any font that looks cute or "fun." This book uses Garamond font for the main text.
- Font size: For the main text, use 11- or 12-point font size. Smaller fonts can be hard to read, and larger fonts look juvenile. This book uses 11-point font for the main text.
- Paragraph spacing and indenting: Use either first-line indents (of 1/2 or 1/4 inch) or extra white space between paragraphs, not both. This book uses white space and no first-line indents.
- Justification: Use left justification (ragged right edge) for draft documents, documents submitted to publishers, and academic documents. Use full justification (smooth right and left edges) for final published documents. This book uses full justification, though not in numbered and bulleted lists.
- Page margins: Use 1-inch margins around the text unless the text will be published in print form, in which case use an extra 1/2 inch margin on the binding side of the page.

Unless otherwise required, for all academic papers and documents submitted for publisher review, use

- 12-point Times New Roman (or equivalent) for all text,
- Double spacing for all text,

- 1/2-inch first line indents,
- No extra space between paragraphs, and
- 1-inch margins around the text.

These specifications give you about 300 words per page, on average.

B. Style Sheets

A style sheet is a list of style specifications. If your document is long and contains many text features, write down the various style details. Doing so will help you follow them consistently. Inconsistent style features will confuse the reader because styles, themselves, communicate something about the content.

C. Automatic Styles

Learn to use the style sheet features on your word processor. I cannot emphasize this strongly enough. Learn to modify pre-existing styles (e.g., heading 1, body text), and learn to create unique styles. You will save much time and trouble, and your text styles will be consistent.

For example, in this book, I modified Heading 1 and Heading 2, and I created styles called "TechWriting Text," "TechWriting Sample," and "TechWriting Bullets." I can select a section of text, click on the appropriate style in the style list, and apply all the style features at once. I use my style sheet to remember which style to apply to which type of text. If I want to change the style for a type of text, I modify the style, and all the text in that style updates automatically. Learn to do this.

19. ONE LAST NOTE: WRITING PROCESS

Step One. Every writing assignment begins the same way, with thinking. Thinking about the reader. Thinking about the purpose. Thinking about the structure. Thinking about the organization. Thinking about the content. Indeed, most writing difficulties stem from a lack of thinking and planning.

Step Two. Outline the content. For shorter documents, you may be able to do this in your mind. For longer, more complex documents, write it down. Your outline may change while you are writing. You may add, combine, move, or, even, remove topics. Regardless, create a plan for what content you will include and how you will organize it.

Step Three. Determine your basic text formatting styles, such as the styles for basic text and headings. Set up the styles in your word processor's style menu.

Step Four. Start writing. Keep writing. You don't have to start at the beginning of the outline, though most people do.

Step Five. Print, read, and revise. You are your first editor and proofreader. Print the entire document and read it carefully. Reading a printed copy is critical. You will review and analyze the document more critically and accurately when reading a printed copy. Consider the content in terms of the readers' needs, and check for mechanics errors. Make changes as necessary.

Step Six. Get a second reader whom you can trust to read carefully, criticize productively, and provide honest feedback.

Step Seven. Make revisions, as necessary, based on Step Six.

Step Eight. Finalize formatting (page size, margins, page breaks, text styles, etc. Update tables of contents.

Step Nine. Print and read aloud. This is your final proofread. Reading aloud is the most accurate way to analyze the text, both for content and for mechanics.

Step Ten. Send it to your copy editor or other professional for review, proofreading, and editing. A professional editor is trained to make your document superior. I highly recommend doing this if the document is important.

Step Eleven. Submit the document to the professor, publisher, readers, etc. You're done. Congratulations!